EVERY VALLEY

EVERY VALLEY

Advent with the Scriptures of Handel's *Messiah*

Compiled by Jessica Miller Kelley

WESTMINSTER
JOHN KNOX PRESS
LOUISVILLE • KENTUCKY

First Edition
Published by Westminster John Knox Press
Louisville, Kentucky

14 15 16 17 18 19 20 21 22 23—10 9 8 7 6 5 4 3 2 1

Book design by Drew Stevens
Cover design by LeVann Fisher Design
Cover illustration: Fantastic evening winter landscape
© Creative Travel Projects/shutterstock.com

Library of Congress Cataloging-in-Publication Data
Every valley : Advent with the scriptures of Handel's Messiah / edited by Jessica Miller Kelley. -- First edition.
   pages cm
   ISBN 978-0-664-25998-3 (alk. paper)
1. Advent--Meditations. 2. Handel, George Frideric, 1685-1759. Messiah. I. Kelley, Jessica Miller, editor.
   BV40.E85 2014
   242'.332--dc23
                                                                  2014004506

PRINTED IN THE UNITED STATES OF AMERICA

♾ The paper used in this publication meets the minimum requirements of the American National Standard for Information Sciences—Permanence of Paper for Printed Library Materials, ANSI Z39.48-1992

CONTENTS

PART 2: CHRIST'S PASSION AND RESURRECTION

PART 3: CHRIST'S ETERNAL REIGN

FOREWORD

"What did the Holy Spirit do," St. Basil asked in the fourth century, "seeing that the human race was not easily led to virtue?" He answers, "The Spirit mixed doctrine with gladdening song, so that when hearing its agreeable and attractive eloquence we might unwittingly learn things beneficial."* So it happened to me as a boy, sixteen centuries after Basil. From Handel's musical settings I unwittingly learned words of the prophets and psalms of Hebrew Scripture, from which *Messiah* takes three-quarters of its texts. In fact I learned from Handel all too well. I was in college before I discovered that the worth of biblical prophecy far exceeds the single dimension presupposed by Handel and his librettist—namely, predicting Jesus as God's Messiah.

The forty reflections in this volume help us appreciate multiple dimensions of *Messiah*'s texts. Biblical prophets looked forward, yes, but the events they anticipated were usually not distant but imminent: Babylonian threat or return from exile (see chap. 1). The prophets observed laterally as well. They examined their contemporary cultures, and with their resounding prefix "Thus saith the Lord!"

* Saint Basil of Caesarea, *Sermon on Psalm 30* (Psalm 29, Septuagint) in *Sancti Patris Nostri Basilii Caesareae Cappadociae...Opera Omnia quae Exstant* (Paris: Apud Gaume Fratres, 1839),1:127. My translation from the Greek. See James W. McKinnon, *Music in Early Christian Literature* (Cambridge: Cambridge University Press, 1987), 65.

they rebuked and warned, corrected and encouraged (see chap. 2). The prophets also steered from behind. Repeatedly in the Gospels we see that the prophets were rudders for the course of Jesus' life, as with the words from Isaiah that Jesus quotes in his self-description: "Go and tell John what you hear and see: the blind receive their sight, the lame walk, the lepers are cleansed, the deaf hear, the dead are raised, and the poor have good news brought to them" (Matt. 11:2–5; see chap. 14).

And with perennial timeliness, prophetic words permeate Jewish, Christian, and Muslim tradition, directing and inspiring the faithful of every age. The reflections in this collection help us comprehend biblical prophecy in its theological, historical, and pastoral dimensions.

Likewise these Advent reflections illumine the New Testament texts of Handel's *Messiah*. The themes of Advent span from preparation for Christ's coming to preparation for Christ's second coming. So also the themes of *Messiah*, which opens with prophecies of Isaiah and ends with the book of Revelation. The season of Advent begins the church's new year, and these reflections on the complete *Messiah* offer us opportunities for contemplating liturgical themes for the twelve months ahead.

All these biblical texts are wonderfully highlighted by Handel's musical settings. His music brings us pleasure and at the same time renders the words indelible in our memories. Sir Kenneth Clark has said that Handel's *Messiah* "is, like Michelangelo's *Creation of Adam*, one of those rare works that appeal immediately to everyone, and yet is indisputably a masterpiece of the highest order."* Many ingredients contribute to *Messiah*'s immediate appeal. The

---

* Kenneth Clark, *Civilisation: A Personal View* (New York: Harper and Row, 1969), 231.

melodies are clear, distinctive, and various. Almost always the texts are presented by a solo voice or a four-part chorus. Handel does not employ vocal duets or quartets where denser textures would tend to obscure the words, and I marvel at the textual transparency of his choral writing. His orchestral accompaniments do not dominate or compete with their texts. (The one exception is movement 48, "The Trumpet Shall Sound," where Handel yields to the inevitability of flourishes from a solo trumpet.)

Another significant feature of Handel's music is less apparent, though once recognized it can heighten *Messiah's* appeal. This ingredient is Handel's skill at "tonal painting"— writing music that echoes the literal meaning of a theme or text. We hear numerous examples in movements 1–3. The instrumental overture that opens *Messiah* closes on a somber chord in E-minor; then movement 2 opens in E-major. The minor-to-major change is like a freshening breeze. Repeating chords played by the strings are tender and welcoming. Handel is painting a tonal background for the words from Isaiah that the tenor is about to sing: "Comfort ye my people."

Tonal painting that pertains to specific words or phrases is often called "word painting." Movements 2 and 3 provide a rich sampler. "Comfort ye": the tenor sings these words on a gently descending phrase and on a third iteration calmly prolongs the first syllable over complete stillness in the orchestra. "And cry unto her that her warfare is accomplished": here the tenor leaps upward an octave for "cry" and sings "accomplished" on a definitive downward close or cadence. "Every valley shall be exalted": the tenor sings "exalted," in the second iteration of that word, on a swirling, continually ascending pattern that encompasses an astonishing forty-eight notes. "And every mountain and hill made low": in the first iteration of this phrase "mountain and hill" are twin melodic summits—one higher and peaked alongside one lower and rounded. And "low" is low.

Descriptions such as this can make word painting seem fussy and distracting. Handel's word painting is so unforced, however, that his music can captivate listeners apart from any awareness of tonal painting. *Messiah* engaged me for years before I became fascinated by Handel's mastery of this musical skill.

We should not expect all of *Messiah* to be as chock-full of word painting as the three opening movements. For one thing the texts of some later movements are more theological and offer less vivid imagery than we find in the words of prophets and psalms. How, for example, might a composer be supposed to paint the text of movement 52: "If God be for us, who can be against us?" Where word painting is ill-suited, tonal painting can nonetheless come into play. The meaning of movement 52 resonates not with musical settings of particular words but with the music's overall mood of sincere graciousness and reverence.

In a letter of 1780 a friend of Handel reported Lord Kinnoull's recollection that upon being congratulated for *Messiah* as a "noble entertainment" for his listeners Handel had replied: "I should be sorry if I only entertained them, I wish to make them better."* The knowing insights of these Advent reflections, combined with the less-witting benefits of what St. Basil calls "gladdening song," help us share in fulfilling that wish for Handel's masterpiece.

Albert L. Blackwell
January 2014

* Otto Erich Deutsch, *Handel: A Documentary Biography* (New York: W. W. Norton, 1954), 855.

EDITOR'S NOTE

For one month a year, at most, the birth of Jesus is placed front and center. Incarnation is singled out for celebration. In contrast, from its earliest days the church made it (at least) a weekly habit to remember the death of Christ. Learning to behold the face of a newborn comes naturally. It takes a lot more practice to take in the full meaning of suffering, death, and eschatological victory.

Reading texts from throughout Christ's story as Christmas approaches helps us to see the full meaning of the incarnation. Special as this season is, liturgically and culturally, Christ's birth must never stand apart from the larger and long story of all that is disclosed to us in Christ—in birth, life, death, atonement, resurrection, and glorification. Though it is typically associated with the Christmas season, Handel's *Messiah* tells the story of Christ through all these phases, with only twenty of fifty-three movements containing traditionally Advent-related themes and texts. But the resurrection focus of the "Hallelujah Chorus" need not render it irrelevant for the Christmas Eve performances we enjoy. In fact, our contemporary celebrations of Christmas, diluted as they can be by commercial hype and the inevitable post-holiday letdown, might be reinvigorated by reflection on the meaning of Christ's advent beyond the manger.

This book offers forty reflections on the Scriptures that comprise the libretto of Handel's *Messiah*. The libretto was written by Charles Jennens, a patron, friend, and collaborator of George Fridric Handel, though for simplicity's sake, only Handel will be referenced in these reflections. Jennens's libretto, taken primarily from the King James text of fourteen books of the Bible, makes *Messiah* a rich source for Bible study and devotion.

Forty, besides being a pleasantly biblical number, just happens to be the maximum number of days there can be in the Advent and Christmas seasons combined. So this book can be used for daily meditation from the start of Advent through the twelfth day of Christmas if the reader so chooses. Alternately, the reader may wish to read each chapter immediately before or after listening to a recording or live performance of *Messiah*.

The entire libretto is covered in this book, with reflections covering as little as part of a movement (if multiple Scriptures are combined in a movement) and as many as three movements (as in chap. 1, which discusses the section of Isaiah 40 from which movements 2–4 are drawn). Each chapter provides a portion of libretto and the same text from the New Revised Standard Version, expanded for context when appropriate, followed by a reflection on the text's historical or theological significance and its potential meaning for the reader's faith and discipleship.

Our hope is that by exploring the Scriptures that make up this beloved oratorio, your experience of Advent, the Bible, and Handel's *Messiah* are all enhanced and that your year-round faith is deepened as a result.

PART 1

CHRIST'S BIRTH
AND ITS FORETELLING

Chapter 1
COMFORT YE MY PEOPLE
(Isaiah 40:1–5)

1. Sinfonia [Overture]

2. Accompanied Recitative

Tenor
Comfort ye, comfort ye my people, saith your God.
Speak ye comfortably to Jerusalem,
and cry unto her,
that her warfare is accomplished,
that her iniquity is pardoned.
The voice of him that crieth in the wilderness;
prepare ye the way of the Lord;
make straight in the desert a highway for our God.

(Isa. 40:1–3)

3. Air

Tenor
Ev'ry valley shall be exalted,
and ev'ry mountain and hill made low;
the crooked straight and the rough places plain.

(Isa. 40:4)

4. Chorus

And the glory of the Lord shall be revealed,
and all flesh shall see it together:
for the mouth of the Lord hath spoken it.

(Isa. 40:5)

Isaiah 40:1–5

[1]Comfort, O comfort my people,
    says your God.
[2]Speak tenderly to Jerusalem,
    and cry to her
that she has served her term,
    that her penalty is paid,
that she has received from the LORD's hand
    double for all her sins.

[3]A voice cries out:
"In the wilderness prepare the way of the LORD,
    make straight in the desert a highway for our God.
[4]Every valley shall be lifted up,
    and every mountain and hill be made low;
the uneven ground shall become level,
    and the rough places a plain."
[5]Then the glory of the LORD shall be revealed,
    and all people shall see it together,
    for the mouth of the LORD has spoken."

Who can think of this text without hearing "Comfort ye, comfort ye, my people" or a precise "Ev'ry valley" from Handel's *Messiah* rendered in a crystal-clear tenor's voice? It may seem at first that this text has been worn so thin that it sounds quaint, just another decoration for the holiday season. Closer study will show that it is a bold declaration about the character of God offered to a demoralized people. Picture the scene. The God of Israel has assembled a heavenly host. This is no council of bickering gods but servants of the sovereign of the universe, whose compassion and regard for justice distinguish this God from other gods. At issue is the situation of God's children, the people of Israel, exiled in Babylon. We can hardly imagine their misery, unless we think of peoples of the earth in our own time who share their agony—refugees from war-torn lands or victims kidnapped and trafficked into modern-day slavery. Stripped of the institutional structures that shaped their lives, their temple destroyed, their homeland laid waste, the people of Israel languish under the thumb of Marduk, the Babylonian god.

God responds to such conditions by bringing together the council. He is prepared to announce a message that God intends for the people of Israel. In it, one can see into the very depths of the character of the one the church calls "Sovereign." God wills comfort and consolation to those in the very depths of despair and depends on human as well as divine agency to bring that message from God's royal realm.

We tend to think of ourselves only as the recipients of these words from on high. We like to cast ourselves as the shepherds who hear the choirs of angels broadcast the startling announcement of God's coming as warrior and shepherd. Surely we do need to hear these ancient words again and again, to be reassured that the God in whom we trust does indeed honor promises and covenants. As we enter the Advent season with various strains and burdens on our hearts, we find solace in tradition and in the timeless language of divine consolation.

But these words are not just for us to savor like food at a holiday feast. We are also in the situation of the celestial ones and the prophets in the text, trying to find a way to speak these words to others whom God loves. One of the questions that leaps up from the text is "What shall I cry?" Presumably it is the prophet's voice, as the prophet tries to understand how to formulate the message that God intends. The prophet uses the imagery and idioms of the time to proclaim that God's glory has been, is being, and will be revealed in the natural order and in the unfolding of human history, a dramatic display of God's certain compassion and care for those who receive it.

To those whose ears are not tuned to this divine doxology, the message is preposterous. It seems clear to some that this God being touted has been defeated by the stronger god of the reigning empire. How is one to take seriously the claim that this God will appear in glory?

Take a look at our own world, and see how preposterous the message we carry will sound. It does indeed seem that the God of Israel and of Jesus Christ has very little power in relation to the other "gods" that seem to reign in our "empire." Particularly during this time of year, approaching Christmas, consumerism demands more of our resources, and lust for oil and mobility threatens our environment. The conduct of war robs us of precious lives and international respect. Religious zealotry pits one image of God against another, leaving the human community fractured and cynical. How dare we speak of this God who promises to become present in a way that "all people shall see it together"?

That is precisely what the faithful people of God are being commissioned to do. In the face of derision and indifference, we are to speak of this God whose fierce compassion and care for humankind trumps the power of the other "gods" who seem to enjoy sovereignty in human relationships.

Advent is a time to hear the promises spoken or sung to the community of faith once again and then sit with them through the season. It is also a time for that community to find its own voice, overcome its objections, and speak words of comfort and assurance to anyone who feels separated or abandoned by God so that God will arrive and will come in gentle power.

Chapter 2

I WILL SHAKE ALL NATIONS
(Haggai 2:1–9)

5. Accompanied Recitative (Part 1)

Bass
Thus saith the Lord, the Lord of hosts;
Yet once a little while and I will shake
the heavens and the earth,
the sea and the dry land.
And I will shake all nations;
and the desire of all nations shall come.
(Hag. 2:6–7)

Haggai 2:1–9

[1]In the seventh month, on the twenty-first day of the month, the word of the LORD came by the prophet Haggai, saying: [2]Speak now to Zerubbabel son of Shealtiel, governor of Judah, and to Joshua son of Jehozadak, the high priest, and to the remnant of the people, and say, [3]Who is left among you that saw this house in its former glory? How does it look to you now? Is it not in your sight as nothing? [4]Yet now take courage, O Zerubbabel, says the LORD; take courage, O Joshua, son of Jehozadak, the high priest; take courage, all you people of the land, says the LORD;

work, for I am with you, says the LORD of hosts,
⁵according to the promise that I made you when you
came out of Egypt. My spirit abides among you; do
not fear. ⁶For thus says the LORD of hosts: Once again,
in a little while, I will shake the heavens and the earth
and the sea and the dry land; ⁷and I will shake all the
nations, so that the treasure of all nations shall come,
and I will fill this house with splendor, says the LORD
of hosts. ⁸The silver is mine, and the gold is mine,
says the LORD of hosts. ⁹The latter splendor of this
house shall be greater than the former, says the LORD
of hosts; and in this place I will give prosperity, says
the LORD of hosts.

To think of the past as a better and perhaps more glorious
time than the present seems to be a common human tendency. We may glorify the era in which we were children
(of course it seemed like a simpler time!), or a particularly
happy phase of life, or perhaps even a time before we were
born. Prophet Haggai and his contemporaries apparently
fell prey to this kind of thinking too.

The outcome of the work of restoring the temple in
Jerusalem after returning from exile was quite disappoint-
ing, when not frustrating, to those of the small nation of
Judah. Back in their land after decades in Babylon, the people were trying hard to bring back the presumed glories of
their preexilic past, but nothing had gone as expected with
the restoration work.

For Haggai's contemporaries, a less-than-perfect
temple was nothing in comparison with their image of
what the temple had looked like during those better times
in the past. That "nothingness," the result of their current

efforts, was acknowledged by the prophet himself, but not without a bit of irony and surprise. "Who is left among you that saw this house in its former glory?" Haggai asks. (The expected answer is, of course, "Nobody," or at most only a few elderly members of the community.) "How does it look to you now? Is it not in your sight as nothing?" (2:3).

Humans generally look for someone to be responsible for a failure, someone to carry the blame for the rest of the group. In this regard, we are no better than our biblical predecessors. If we cannot find someone among us, then the next obvious candidate is God, as happens so often in the Scripture. After all, should not God know or fare better than we? If God does not do better than we do, then what does it mean to be God? Surely God knows well the people's frustration as well as their complaint.

It is to this context that Haggai declares that God is with them, even if it is not quite obvious, working with and through them, and that God will make himself known. This affirmation of God's presence and support alone should give them courage. It is God's promise to the people. Not even the most difficult circumstances for the most arduous task will persuade God to stay away. Actually, staying away or being unconcerned is not in the nature of this God. Whatever it takes to help the people out, God is able and willing to do, even if it means shaking "the heavens and the earth . . . the sea and the dry land; and . . . all the nations" (2:6–7).

God will provide what the people need for the task at hand. The resources they need to rebuild and restore the temple will come from other lands. It is another sign that God is God above all nations. The treasures of the earth, as well as the accumulated goods of other nations, fall under God's active rule. The spirit of God moves and goes anywhere, abiding where God wants it to. This abiding spirit is the promise of divine presence and initiative among the people.

And this brings us to one of the basic tenets of Haggai's theological thinking: the presence of God is evident in the glory of God, which is where the real glory of Haggai's people lies as well (not in the former glory of the temple). Without the glory of the divine presence, all attempts at national rebuilding will come to naught. Never mind about how things look or do not look, Haggai says. Concern yourselves instead about whether God has decided to make God's presence felt among you. Either the spirit abides or the spirit does not abide. The spirit dwells where God decides it will.

The task ahead might be truly uphill, but God through the spirit will be with and for the rebuilders. The spirit will abide with the people so that the temple's—and hence the nation's—"latter splendor . . . shall be greater than the former." Within this concrete place, God will show what only God can do and wishes to accomplish. Divine presence is the glory of the people.

For a people who have been downtrodden for a long time and whose hopes have all but disappeared, the assurance of such divine presence is quite uplifting, to say the least. Here we have a small remnant of a nation, a people with almost no resources except for themselves and their faith. In the midst of utter despair, they can hear a gracious word of affirmation as a people from the one who matters the most: their God, the Lord of hosts. Now they have not only God's spirit but also God's word to go with them.

Chapter 3
HE SHALL COME
(Malachi 2:13–3:1)

5. Accompanied Recitative (Part 2)

Bass
The Lord, whom ye seek,
shall suddenly come to His temple,
even the messenger of the Covenant,
whom you delight in;
behold, He shall come,
saith the Lord of hosts.

(Mal. 3:1)

Malachi 2:13–14a, 17–3:1

[13]You cover the LORD's altar with tears, with weeping and groaning because he no longer regards the offering or accepts it with favor at your hand. [14]You ask, "Why does he not?" ...

[17]You have wearied the LORD with your words. Yet you say, "How have we wearied him?" By saying, "All who do evil are good in the sight of the Lord, and he delights in them." Or by asking, "Where is the God of justice?"

[3:1]See, I am sending my messenger to prepare the way before me, and the Lord whom you seek will suddenly come to his temple. The messenger of the covenant in whom you delight—indeed, he is coming, says the LORD of hosts.

*W*hen Elie Weisel, the Jewish writer and Nobel Prize winner, was a boy, his mother would greet him every day when he returned from school. Each day she would ask him the same question. She did not ask, "What did you do today?" or "Whom did you talk to today?" or even "What did you learn today?" She would ask, "Did you have a good question today?"

Malachi had some good questions for his day: "'How have you [God] loved us?'" (1:2); "Has not one God created us?" (2:10); "'Where is the God of justice?'" (2:17); "'How shall we return [to God]?'" (3:7). Malachi poses twenty-two questions in just fifty-five verses. God's questions to the priests and the people are articulated; their responses to God are anticipated. Rhetorical questions emphasize the prophetic passion for integrity; direct inquiries evoke the people's questions and provoke impassioned response. The question-and-answer style opens prophetic deliverance to more of a prophet-and-people deliberation, edgy but candid, confrontational and engaging. They are now partners in critical reflection on the nature of God and self-critical reflection on the conduct of the people of Israel.

Malachi has some good questions for our day. His very use of questions as a means of prophetic revelation counters the unthinking certitude of much so-called religious conviction. "Who can endure the day of his coming?" Who will be "pure and blameless" in the day of Christ? Who will prepare the way by repentance and forgiveness?

Advent questions! Advent questions our worthiness, readiness, and willingness for Christ's coming.

A faithful hearing of this text may invite us to ask certain questions of ourselves during Advent: Are our prayers prophetic as well as personal, directed to injustice and corruption as well as seasonal anxiety and individual omissions? Do our songs acknowledge the messenger's judgment as well as the joy of coming incarnation? While many are eager to sing and hear the familiar Christmas carols, Advent hymns contain themes that are discordant and somber. Uncomfortable as it may be, however, Advent calls us to venture into these uncomfortable places with questions like "How have we wearied him?" and to face head on the possibility that we have wearied the Lord in some of the same ways Malachi's audience had: by convincing ourselves that evil is good or by shirking our own responsibility for the world's ills by asking, "Where is the God of justice?"

The people to whom Malachi speaks are skeptical of God's justice because their practices of piety have yielded neither divine retributive judgment against "evil-doers" nor prosperity for the restoration community. Their challenges to the prophet smack of self-righteousness, and they seemingly have failed to notice that their compromised worship practices, marital infidelity, and social injustice dishonor God. They seek and desire the coming of the Lord, imagining that it will be favorable for them. They ask where God is with the smug presumption that he is far off.

Malachi responds with assurance that God's appearance is imminent. "See, I am sending my messenger to prepare the way . . . he is coming" (3:1). He shall come, but be aware, the prophet reminds us, that the arrival of divine judgment rarely meets human expectations. It is sudden, surprising, and often as much a judgment against the ones yearning for it as it is a judgment against their enemies.

After the first presentation of *Messiah* in London in 1743, Handel wrote to a friend, "I should be sorry if I only entertained them. I wish to make them better."* The composer challenges us to go beyond feeling good to doing good. Is our Advent devotion about entertainment or edification? Diversion or direction? Amusement or awareness? Handel himself provided an answer. Although by 1751 he was blind, until his death he conducted *Messiah* as an annual benefit for the Foundling Hospital in London, which served mostly widows and orphans of the clergy. The intent was not just to entertain; Handel's hope was to make the audience just and better. Our expectation of the Messiah's coming is incomplete without awareness of our own need for justice.

---

* Otto Erich Deutsch, *Handel: A Documentary Biography* (New York: W. W. Norton, 1954), 855.

Chapter 4
AND HE SHALL PURIFY
(Malachi 3:2–4)

6. Air

Alto
But who may abide the day of His coming,
and who shall stand when He appeareth?
For He is like a refiner's fire.

(Mal. 3:2)

7. Chorus

And He shall purify the sons of Levi,
that they may offer unto the Lord
an offering in righteousness.

(Mal. 3:3)

Malachi 3:2–4

²But who can endure the day of his coming, and who can stand when he appears?

For he is like a refiner's fire and like fullers' soap; ³he will sit as a refiner and purifier of silver, and he will purify the descendants of Levi and refine them like gold and silver, until they present offerings to the LORD in righteousness. ⁴Then the offering of Judah

16

and Jerusalem will be pleasing to the LORD as in the days of old and as in former years.

*T*he word of the Lord came to Malachi as a word of promise. That promise comes as good news to us, but there is also at least a degree of uneasiness in the promise. There are some elements of the promise that we would love to have fulfilled and other elements that we would just as soon leave unfulfilled.

The prophet describes the Lord's coming as like the refiner's fire, whose purpose is to remove impurities and strengthen the substance being refined. John Calvin wrote this about the refiner's fire: "The power of the fire, we know, is twofold: for it burns and it purifies; it burns what is corrupt; but it purifies gold and silver from their dross."*

The believer responds to this promise by wondering exactly what is meant by the refining. What exactly in my life is in need of refining? And how much will it hurt? What might I have to give up (or what might be taken from me) before I would be refined like gold and silver?

In many ways, our response to this text is probably not that much different from the response of Malachi's original audience. Like them, we want to stand and see that day. We want our offerings to be pleasing to the Lord. We want to see the restoration of the covenant. We want to see things made right, the way God intended—and yet, we are not so sure. We do not want to go through too much change or pain to see it happen.

What is it that stands in need of purification? And what will be consumed by flames in the process? After

---

* John Calvin, *Commentaries on the Twelve Minor Prophets*, ed. and trans. John Owen (Grand Rapids: Eerdmans, 1950), 5:573.

purification, what is it that God reckons as precious metal?
When God's promise, spoken through Malachi, is finally
fulfilled, what will look different in our world and our lives?
As we ask these questions, however, we must guard against
using Malachi as an occasion to attack enemies or to point
out all the things that some imagined "they" are doing
wrong. Rather, *we* are the ones who are going to be refined.
We are the ones in need of refining.

Frightful as it may sound, there is comfort to be found
in this process of refining. Contrary to popular understand-
ings of the judgment that awaits each of us, the image presented here is not a stark binary between worthy wheat and
unworthy chaff. Rather, the wheat and chaff grow together
within each of us, like the raw gold ore with all its impurities. The refining fire burns away what is unworthy in us
and purifies what is good, making us a worthy and pleasing
offering to the Lord when we appear before him.

Purification has another possible purpose in addition
to the removal of impurities. When silver is refined, it is
treated with carbon or charcoal, preventing the absorption
of oxygen and resulting in its sheen and purity. One writer
has suggested that a silversmith knows that the refining process is complete only when she observes her "own image
reflected in the mirror-like surface of the metal."* If this is
the case, does the prophet also suggest that the *imago Dei*
is restored in this process? Is humanity deemed good and
righteous when once again the divine image is reflected in
the human heart?

There may be questions regarding the process, but
the promise of this restoration and refining is sure. It will

* Ralph L. Smith, *Micah-Malachi*, Word Bible Commentary 32 (Waco, TX: Word
Books, 1984), 329.

happen, and it will happen under God's control and in God's time. The refining is not waiting for us to feel good about it. God's promise is sure, and it is good news. We will be re-formed in God's image, and it will be good no matter how we feel about it and no matter what we may be afraid of now. When we are refined and purified as God promises, it will be good.

Chapter 5

GOD WITH US
(Isaiah 7:10–16)

8. Recitative

Alto
Behold, a virgin shall conceive
and bear a son, and shall call
His name Emmanuel, God with us.
                    (Isa. 7:14; Matt. 1:23)

Isaiah 7:10–16

[10]Again the Lord spoke to Ahaz, saying, [11]Ask a sign of the Lord your God; let it be deep as Sheol or high as heaven. [12]But Ahaz said, I will not ask, and I will not put the Lord to the test. [13]Then Isaiah said: "Hear then, O house of David! Is it too little for you to weary mortals, that you weary my God also? [14]Therefore the Lord himself will give you a sign. Look, the young woman is with child and shall bear a son, and shall name him Immanuel. [15]He shall eat curds and honey by the time he knows how to refuse the evil and choose the good. [16]For before the child knows how to refuse the evil and choose the good, the land before whose two kings you are in dread will be deserted."

*I*n these treasured and classic words, Isaiah delivers the great sign of God's promise: a young woman will give birth to a son whose name will be Immanuel, "God with us." Our overfamiliarity with words about a virgin's conceiving and bearing a son may lead many to take this claim for granted. On the other hand, the words may also rouse our skepticism about the veracity of Jesus' virgin birth. What can keep us from either presumption or incredulity about the prophet's Advent proclamation of this sign? Perhaps the answer lies in the hidden depth and historical complexity we encounter in Isaiah's sign of the incarnation.

Isaiah comes to reassure King Ahaz that Jerusalem will not be captured by the coalition that has formed against him. The divine intention mediated through the prophet is to thwart the enemies of Jerusalem. Ahaz is offered a sign from God if he but ask for it, but Ahaz refuses, with the excuse that he does not wish to tempt God. This rejection of God's offer betrays his fear and his lack of trust. Even so, Isaiah declares that God will give a sign anyway—a woman pregnant with a child of promise. As it turns out, the child is also a sign of the Assyrian invasion that will devastate Jerusalem. What a strange and disorienting sign to the prophet's hearers!

In our contemporary situation it is problematic to claim that God characteristically operates by raising up and destroying armies, though vestiges of that theological viewpoint are real. The hope for the coming of a child of destiny is also certainly still alive in secular society. In complicated times—politically, socially, economically—the yearning for some sign of promise and hope in the form of a new leader is still very much with us. This is true both outside and inside our churches. Isaiah's Advent sign raises the question of how God enters and acts within the world of time and space.

The particular sign God gives in Isaiah arouses hope. The idea of a child who grows over time into the promise of a world made right is a remarkable image for any idea of human salvation. At the same time it opens up the gap between what the world is and what it ought to be. Such a sign focuses the contrast between the forces arrayed *against* the good and the hope for salvation from all that is violent and destructive. Awareness of the gap between what is and what ought to be kindles the prophetic spirit in every age. As in Isaiah's circumstances, so too in our own.

The vulnerability and the unexpected future of a child borne in a womb and birthed into this world are indispensable features of this sign given in Isaiah's prophecy. On the one hand, there is vulnerability: a child as such is subject to growing up—coming to know evil and good. The apparent weakness of a child plays against the hope. As the words of Johann Rist's chorale "Break Forth O Beauteous Heavenly Light" (used by J. S. Bach in his *Christmas Oratorio*) express it, "This child, now weak in infancy, our joy and confidence shall be." The hearers too are vulnerable to the circumstances that challenge their very existence in the world as it is. Thus an element of "fear and trembling" must accompany the receiving of such a sign.

We characteristically require more certainty than this sign seems to offer. This was true of the situation that Isaiah addressed, but it is true always of the historical situation into which every Advent brings us. The church is called by Advent to face the vulnerabilities of time and place. The very sign by which God promises to world and to church, "I will be with you" evokes the unexpected hope. When

Advent falls in the midst of severe human travail—as it has fallen and will fall again—it is hope against all the evidence.

The sign of a child is to be seen and heard against our deepest fears but also against our desires that the world be transformed. As in the great Advent hymn "O Come, O Come, Immanuel," the ancient biblical images of what God has promised stir us beyond our clichés and our presumptions. The sign God gives, despite our own refusals and our self-interests in deliverance, goes beyond our ambivalences to God's eternal self-consistency. God's covenant with the creation is to redeem it from the inside out. The promise of a messiah is grounded in God's intention to restore us and to transform the world as we have come to make it into our own image. The divine promise is thus deeply hidden in God's own being, just as the child is hidden in the mother's womb.

Chapter 6

O THOU THAT TELLEST GOOD TIDINGS

(Isaiah 40:6–9)

9. Air (Part 1)

Alto

O thou that tellest good tidings to Zion,
get thee up into the high mountain.
O thou that tellest good tidings to Jerusalem,
lift up thy voice with strength;
lift it up, be not afraid; say unto the cities of Judah,
behold your god!

(Isa. 40:9)

Isaiah 40:6–9

[6]A voice says, "Cry out!"
 And I said, "What shall I cry?"
 All people are grass,
 their constancy is like the flower of the field.
[7]The grass withers, the flower fades,
 when the breath of the Lord blows upon it;
 surely the people are grass.
[8]The grass withers, the flower fades;
 but the word of our God will stand forever.
[9]Get you up to a high mountain,
 O Zion, herald of good tidings;

lift up your voice with strength,
O Jerusalem, herald of good tidings,
lift it up, do not fear;
say to the cities of Judah,
"Here is your God!"

*I*n contrast to the words of judgment and warning in the
first thirty-nine chapters of Isaiah (known as First Isaiah, as
it differs significantly from later chapters not only in terms
of historical location and context but also in terms of theological content), Isaiah 40 brings good news about God's
comfort and God's promise of redemption for a people
who have lived in exile for some 150 years. First Isaiah
announces God's judgment by means of Assyria on Israel's
sin. Second Isaiah (chapters 40–55), however, announces
good news or "gospel" about God. The first verses of Isaiah 40 offer "comfort, comfort" to the people and proclaim
that "every valley" will be exalted.

But we should be careful not to read these good tidings apart from Isaiah's first thirty-nine chapters. We must
not separate God's grace and forgiveness from God's judgment on human sin. To do so renders God's grace and forgiveness cheap and capricious and renders God's judgment
on sin sheer retribution. Can human sin be known apart
from God's grace? And can God's grace be known apart
from our sin?

Perhaps this is why a heavenly voice in Isaiah 40:6
commissions a herald, who will bring good tidings within
just a few verses, which begin by reminding the people of
their frailty. "All people are grass," the voice says. We are
weak, fallible, unfaithful. Flesh, grass, and flowers fade and
wither; everything perishes, but "the word of our God will

stand forever." Survivors of disaster know with profound certainty the ephemeral nature of life. Now, in bracing contrast, the prophet assures them of the steady, durable, and reliable foreverness of the divine word.

Once that message of our mortal limitation and God's limitless strength has been made clear, the hearer is prepared for the good news to follow. At verse 9, the herald's instructions come to a climax when she is told to climb to a high mountain. She must go up high to project her voice far and wide as she proclaims the good news, the message of joy. The voice urges her to cry out fearlessly. But what is fearful about her task? Are her words too improbable to be believed by the cities of Judah to whom she is to proclaim it? Are they too hard to speak fearlessly about Judah's new life during Babylonian occupation? Is her joyful news too world-reversing even to be imagined?

It may be hard for us in our modern, first-world context to comprehend the significance of the herald's message. Isaiah presumes that his audience dwells in a country far from home, where they live with much fear and anxiety. In what sense do we hear this promise of comfort as a people that has ceased to pine for home? Most likely, we read only from a cultural captivity that leaves us unconscious of our spiritual exile. The words "Comfort, comfort" ring empty when there is no discomfort among us happy inhabitants of Babylon (readying ourselves for a holiday, no less). Without the context of exile and separation, we may confuse this costly word of comfort with the sentiment of the season.

We need to remember our frailty, our need for God, in order to truly hear the herald's message for ourselves. Honoring the repentant imperative of Advent, we might begin by naming those corporate and personal places of exile that take us far from the God who requires justice and mercy from us. Confessing all the ways we fall short, acknowledging our inconsistency, and recognizing how brief and ultimately insignificant our lives are bring the Lord's glory into stark relief.

"Behold your God," we sing, and by knowing better the reality of our own condition, we can more clearly see this God we behold, this God whose mighty Word alone negates our mortality against its every rival. "Behold your God!" we sing, and with the herald and Handel's chorus, we can lift up our voices with strength, ready to meet the God before us.

Chapter 7

ARISE, SHINE
(Isaiah 60:1–6)

9. Air (Part 2)

Alto

Arise, shine, for thy light is come,
and the glory of the Lord is risen upon thee.

(Isa. 60:1)

10. Accompanied Recitative

Bass

For behold, darkness shall cover the earth,
and gross darkness the people;
but the Lord shall arise upon thee,
and His glory shall be seen upon thee.
And the Gentiles shall come to thy light,
and kings to the brightness of thy rising.

(Isa. 60:2–3)

Isaiah 60:1-6

[1]Arise, shine; for your light has come,
    and the glory of the Lord has risen upon you.
[2]For darkness shall cover the earth,
    and thick darkness the peoples;

but the LORD will arise upon you,
> and his glory will appear over you.
³Nations shall come to your light,
> and kings to the brightness of your dawn.

⁴Lift up your eyes and look around;
> they all gather together, they come to you;
your sons shall come from far away,
> and your daughters shall be carried on their
> nurses' arms.
⁵Then you shall see and be radiant;
> your heart shall thrill and rejoice,
because the abundance of the sea shall be
> brought to you,
> the wealth of the nations shall come to you.
⁶A multitude of camels shall cover you,
> the young camels of Midian and Ephah;
> all those from Sheba shall come.
They shall bring gold and frankincense,
> and shall proclaim the praise of the LORD.

*I*n a time of despair and discouragement, the prophet of Third Isaiah (chapters 56–66) offers more than encouragement; he offers a vision so glorious and compelling that anyone who trusts the Lord will be inspired and motivated to work hard to rebuild and renew the land and the people. The exiles have returned from Babylon, but instead of the welcoming and peaceful homeland of their grandparents' stories, they find ruin, decay, and corruption.

One can almost picture the forlorn returnees in the midst of it all, their lifelong hopes cruelly dashed. When the best of the best were taken from their homeland seventy years

ago, those who were left behind did not have the skills or
qualities required to run the government, educate the young,
or see to the spiritual health of the community. Perhaps those
left behind can hardly be blamed that Israel was not the place
after the exile that it was before, but when the exiles returned
home, they found a mess that they did not expect. Instead
of glory and health, they found crumbling buildings, incom-
petent and corrupt authorities, and a terrible apathy in the
nation's religious practice. The returnees were devastated.
This was not at all what they had set their hopes on.

   In the midst of this grief and desperation, the prophet
speaks an incongruous invitation: "Arise, shine, for your light
has come, and the glory of the LORD has risen upon you"
(60:1). It is perhaps hard to believe, but it does stir memories
of Second Isaiah, the prophet of the exile, who also promised
that the Lord's light would shine in their present darkness
(e.g., chaps. 40 and 43). Darkness is an overarching metaphor
for many ways in which life is difficult and human experience
seems to shut out joy. This is especially true in Second and
Third Isaiah, which are composed of long poetic passages
mourning the darkness of the current circumstances and praying for God's light, which includes both spiritual faithfulness
and material prosperity, to shine once again on God's people.

   The next part of the prophecy offers this hope but, in
the usual way of God, offers so much more than God's people could have asked for or imagined. Not only would God's
glory shine on this forsaken place—this dark place—but it
would shine so brightly that Judah would be envied by the
rest of the world. From far and near, God's own children
would return home, and the days of homelessness, of wandering in the dark among strangers, would be over forever,
because the light of God—again, spiritual faithfulness and
material prosperity—would never be extinguished. There

would be no wandering in the darkness among strangers, because strangers and foreigners would also come to Judah, bringing gifts and wealth and begging to be included in this glorious restoration. Not only would Israel be brought back to its proper glory, but the rest of the world would be drawn to the light that shone only there.

The images of this ingathering hearken back to God's call to Abraham to be a blessing to all the families of the earth. Abraham's homeland will be the gathering place for all God's children, who will come bringing their finest treasures as an offering to God and for the benefit of God's people. For the Christian, these images hearken forward to the redemption of all creation in Jesus Christ—the One who on the cross opens his arms wide to draw all people to himself. However, here in the between times, readers are shown a people willing to be inspired by and work hard for a vision that is, as yet, out of their reach. The proclamation of this passage is one of hope, of something that is promised but for which we are still waiting in faith.

The Revised Common Lectionary has this passage read each year at Epiphany, when the verses envisioning the arrival of foreign worshipers, camels, and strangers bearing gifts of gold and frankincense evoke images of Matthew's Gospel, with its visit of foreign wise men bearing these exact gifts (plus the significant addition of myrrh for burial). In Matthew's theology, the promises of both Second and Third Isaiah are fulfilled in Jesus. But as Matthew Henry says, for believers the promises of God are our starting point, not the end nor even the goal of our life of faith. Knowing what God promises, that "the glory of the LORD has risen upon you," and "the LORD will arise upon you," we begin our journey toward him, bringing our finest gifts and bringing others along with us, until all are gathered to him in the light of his glory.

Chapter 8

THE PEOPLE THAT WALKED IN DARKNESS
(Isaiah 9:1–2)

11. Air

Bass
The people that walked in darkness
have seen a great light;
and they that dwell in the land of the shadow of death,
upon them hath the light shined.

(Isa. 9:2)

Isaiah 9:1-2

¹But there will be no gloom for those who were in anguish. In the former time he brought into contempt the land of Zebulun and the land of Naphtali, but in the latter time he will make glorious the way of the sea, the land beyond the Jordan, Galilee of the nations.
²The people who walked in darkness
   have seen a great light;
those who lived in a land of deep darkness—
   on them light has shined.

*A*dvent begins during the darkest time of the year; the days get shorter and shorter as December wears on, only to halt and reverse (not coincidentally, of course) right before Christmas. Sunlight hours then begin to lengthen, the light remaining with us a little longer each day. The light Isaiah looks toward, however, is not light that grows gradually over time. The brightness of the light Isaiah proclaims shines on a people walking in darkness like a brilliant dawn suddenly breaking. This, surely, is the kind of light that illuminates every secret place, bringing a path obscured by shadows suddenly into view. It is the kind of light that gives direction and drives out fear.

Isaiah speaks his prophecy of light into a moment of tremendous fear for the people of Israel, a time of "distress and darkness, the gloom of anguish" (Isa. 8:22). Assyrian invaders have attacked the northern kingdom, shearing away portions of Israel to create Assyrian provinces. The oracle in Isaiah 9 reflects the oppressive military occupation under which Israel struggles to live. Isaiah speaks his word of light and hope into a time of desolation.

As he waits in the darkness of cruelty and oppression, Isaiah imagines and proclaims that the light of God's face will again shine on the people of Israel. Do not be afraid, Isaiah seems to say. Do not give up. God's light will break through our gloom and anguish, scattering it. Isaiah sings a song of liberation into the darkness, a song of the God who lifts the burdensome yoke under which the people are trapped.

It takes courage to preach hope in the midst of such desolation. Courage, or a dangerous naiveté. For preaching hope can be done badly, hurtfully. When people are living in "the gloom of anguish," a word of hope too easily spoken can leave that anguish unacknowledged, deepening the pain. Isaiah does not speak carelessly, however. Nor does he speak as one who can afford to hope because he is exempt from the suffering he addresses. Isaiah speaks as part of the community, one of the people who walk in darkness. He speaks with authority, passion, and confidence that God is still present.

Many scholars believe that the oracle in Isaiah 9 celebrates the ascension of Hezekiah to "the throne of David and his kingdom" (Isa. 9:7). Certainly Isaiah's words celebrate with joy the new king in whom so much hope is invested, but he celebrates the king in words that transcend the accomplishments of any particular leader, words that express the deepest longings of his community. Isaiah's oracle keeps before his listeners and his readers the vision of a day when the life of the world will be shaped by justice and righteousness and blessed by a peace that will never end.

Isaiah reminds us of the importance of imagination in faith, the capacity to see beyond things as they are and to imagine things as they might be. He reminds us not to lower our sights, not to get comfortable with the status quo, not to be satisfied with anything less than the release of those held captive, the end of war making, and the lifting of the burden of oppression from all peoples everywhere. Long after the memory of Hezekiah's accomplishments, and his compromises, has faded into the past, Isaiah's vision of what is possible continues to inspire the fiercest hopes of human beings for the future. Even in a time of desolation, Isaiah is able to imagine and to describe a great light breaking, illuminating the path of those who walk in darkness, fear, and pain.

Where that path leads, as later passages in Isaiah proclaim, is outward: outward to the coastlands, outward to the ends of the great, wide world. Isaiah not only promises that God's people will be given a light to see by and a light to walk by; he promises that following that light will lead them ever more deeply into the life of the world. To those who have been waiting for God's light to break in upon their darkness, God says, "I will give you as a light to the nations, that my salvation may reach to the end of the earth" (Isa. 49:6).

Isaiah reminds us that God intends those on whom God's light shines to be themselves a gift, "a light to the nations." Isaiah reminds us that we are called to share the light we can see and feel. We are also called, like Isaiah, to share the light that we can only yet imagine.

Chapter 9

FOR UNTO US
A CHILD IS BORN
(Isaiah 9:3–7)

12. Chorus

For unto us a child is born,
unto us a son is given,
and the government shall be upon His shoulder;
and His name shall be called Wonderful,
Counsellor, the mighty God, the Everlasting Father,
the Prince of Peace.

(Isa. 9:6)

Isaiah 9:3–7

[3]You have multiplied the nation,
    you have increased its joy;
they rejoice before you
    as with joy at the harvest,
    as people exult when dividing plunder.
[4]For the yoke of their burden,
    and the bar across their shoulders,
    the rod of their oppressor,
    you have broken as on the day of Midian.
[5]For all the boots of the tramping warriors
    and all the garments rolled in blood
    shall be burned as fuel for the fire.

⁶For a child has been born for us,
    a son given to us;
authority rests upon his shoulders;
    and he is named
Wonderful Counselor, Mighty God,
    Everlasting Father, Prince of Peace.
⁷His authority shall grow continually,
    and there shall be endless peace
for the throne of David and his kingdom.
He will establish and uphold it
with justice and with righteousness
    from this time onward and forevermore.
The zeal of the LORD of hosts will do this.

*T*hese memorable words can easily be heard in a kind of sentimental haze, familiar from countless Christmas Eve services as well as from Handel's stunning presentation of the messianic titles: "Wonderful Counselor, Mighty God, Everlasting Father, Prince of Peace." In this beloved passage, Isaiah brings an astounding claim: God has come to the world in the form of a boy child born of a young woman. It is no wonder that this reading has been associated with Christmas through the centuries. It is no wonder that this reading is also heard as the culmination of prophetic desire for a messiah.

The announcement of a world-transforming reign of righteousness and justice now begun is not a sentimental set of feeling states. It is a radical prophetic claim. To someone on the edges of the Christian faith, it may seem impossibly hopeful, even naive. "Endless peace"? Really? "Justice with righteousness"? Where?

Any honest dealing with Isaiah 9:3–7 will have to acknowledge that the prophecy is as yet unfulfilled. Like John the Baptist, we may look at these prophesies, look at Jesus, and ask, " 'Are you the one who is to come, or are we to wait for another?' " (Matt. 11:3). Underlying the question is the messianic expectation that one will come to fix everything. It is that expectation that Jesus does not meet. Jesus is not a messiah who solves all problems and makes it unnecessary for us to do the hard work of peacemaking or establishing justice or righteousness. The text is subversive, contradicting what we imagine is the way the world has to work and inviting us to imagine the world as God intends it. Why is the world not the way God intends it?

Neither Isaiah nor the New Testament suggests that the light does away with the darkness (see John 1:5). Yet the light of Christ has proved to be tough and tenacious. We can trust that the light of God's goodness and grace continues to shine in spite of the world's dark realities, and we can be confident in approaching Christ with whatever darkness is within ourselves. This paradox is the very definition of hope—to see the potential of light in places where we may now only see darkness.

Isaiah illustrates this hope by speaking in the present tense ("unto us a child is born") of that which is still in the future. What kind of sign is this that has been or will be fulfilled? Such a vulnerable sign—utterly human in its appearance but with the power to alter human destiny! This is the divine counterpoint to all human powers and principalities: a child born who transforms the violence; images of violence that are themselves subverted by the child. This proclamation turns darkness into an illumination of the way of justice, peace, and righteousness. This is hope incarnate.

How is this possible? Not by mere human engineer-
ing. Only by the very passion of God, Isaiah asserts, for the
"zeal of the LORD of hosts" will do this (v. 7). As armies rage
against one another, the Lord of hosts, literally "Lord of the
armies," will rise up in zeal to bring the end of all war.

The period in which Isaiah writes, a period of
encroaching Assyrian domination and fear in the hearts of
the people, has much in common with the time of Jesus'
birth, when Judah is a resident captive of Rome, and Herod,
who is not in the line of David, sits on the throne in Jerusalem. The people in both periods long for a powerful sign
that God will redeem them from oppression, and the birth
of a baby seems hardly the great sign they have awaited.
But looked at in another way, this sign of new life is not
ordinary at all. It is a sign that only the Creator God can
give. It is the sign promised to Abraham and Sarah (Gen.
12–21). It was the sign that the midwives protected during
the Egyptian captivity (Exod. 1). It was the sign of God's
promise offered to Ahaz (Isa. 7:14). What is a more fitting
sign of God's love than the creation of a new life, even in the
midst of a broken world? It is no wonder that this new baby
will be named Jesus, meaning, "the Lord saves." God's sign
of love for the world is now God's own Son, born so that
the world might be saved.

Chapter 10
KEEPING WATCH
(Luke 2:8–10)

13. Pastoral Symphony

14a. Recitative

Soprano
There were shepherds abiding in the field,
keeping watch over their flocks by night.
(Luke 2:8)

14b. Accompanied Recitative

Soprano
And lo, the angel of the Lord came upon them,
and the glory of the Lord shone round about them,
and they were sore afraid.
(Luke 2:9)

15. Recitative (Part 1)

Soprano
And the angel said unto them,
"Fear not, for behold,
I bring you good tidings of great joy,
which shall be to all people."
(Luke 2:10)

Luke 2:8-10

[8]In that region there were shepherds living in the fields, keeping watch over their flock by night. [9]Then an angel of the Lord stood before them, and the glory of the Lord shone around them, and they were terrified. [10]But the angel said to them, "Do not be afraid; for see—I am bringing you good news of great joy for all the people."

*H*andel makes his transition to the New Testament not with the annunciation to Mary or even Jesus' birth in Luke 2:7, but with the following verses in which angels appear to a group of shepherds working near Bethlehem.

By appearing to shepherds, God showed God's willingness to appear to any who will listen. God came unexpectedly, at night, to those who were simply going about their daily occupations. The shepherds had not withdrawn from the world to seek holiness; they were simply going about their tasks, and God appeared. The shepherds were probably tired, tending sheep at night. Then, unexpectedly and intrusively, God's messenger appeared. The angels terrified them. The shepherds had apparently not been waiting or praying for a message. But nonetheless, the angel interrupts their ordinary lives with the declaration " 'I am bringing you good news.' "

Before jumping to the conclusion that "you" simply means *us*—us hearers, whoever we might be—it might behoove us to investigate. To whom is this good news addressed?

It is not insignificant that the good news is brought to shepherds. Shepherds were held in low esteem in those days; they lived outside the boundaries of polite society, were assumed to lead shiftless lives, and were smelly, dirty, and crude. They would have been regarded with some suspicion by respectable folk and would hardly be considered trustworthy sources for any news of import. And yet they are the first to hear, the first to see, the first to tell of Jesus' birth. The angel did not appear to kings or prelates but to those of low status, the sorts of people with whom Jesus would come to associate in his ministry.

Writing to Christians in Corinth, Paul indicates that this is God's way:

> Consider your own call, brothers and sisters: not many of you were wise by human standards, not many were powerful, not many were of noble birth. But God chose what is foolish in the world to shame the wise; God chose what is weak in the world to shame the strong; God chose what is low and despised in the world, things that are not, to reduce to nothing things that are.
>
> (1 Cor. 1:26–28)

This theme is reflected over and over in the Lukan Christmas narrative: in the annunciation to Mary, in her Magnificat, in the mean circumstances of Jesus' birth, in the calling of the shepherds to see and tell. It is in Luke's Gospel that Jesus identifies himself as the one "anointed," in the words of Isaiah,

> " to bring good news to the poor.
> . . . to proclaim release to the captives
> and recovery of sight to the blind,
> to let the oppressed go free."
>
> (Luke 4:18)

But fitting as this gospel to the lowly is, the news the angel brings is not just for the shepherds: "'I am bringing you good news of great joy for all the people'" (2:10). Surely we are among "'all the people,'" right? The King James Version (and thus, Handel) says simply "all people," eliminating any confusion that might arise from an implied distinction: *the* people, as in some particular people, the people of X as distinct from other people, or perhaps "the common people" as distinct from "the rulers" or "the clergy." If the angel is being specific here, are we then among "the people" to whom this good news is spoken? Perhaps the answer to that question, on some level, is up to us. Will we receive this good news with great joy? To those of us already claiming the Christian faith, so many centuries after the angel's pronouncement, to respond with joy seems obvious. But such a response may be more complicated than we initially think. If Jesus is born and anointed to "'proclaim release to the captives,'" this may not exactly seem like good news to the captors, nor to those who have profited by the poverty of the poor. Luke is the Gospel of a rich fool (12:13–21), the rich man who neglects Lazarus to his peril (16:19–31), and the all-too-direct words of Jesus: "'Woe to you who are rich, for you have received your consolation'" (Luke 6:24).

Will Christ's coming mean joy or woe for us? We must look at our own lives to see what the good news means for us and how we will respond to it.

Chapter 11

BORN THIS DAY
(Luke 2:11–12)

15. Recitative (Part 2)

Soprano
"For unto you is born this day
in the city of David a Saviour,
which is Christ the Lord."
(Luke 2:11)

Luke 2:11–12

[11]"To you is born this day in the city of David a Savior, who is the Messiah, the Lord. [12]This will be a sign for you: you will find a child wrapped in bands of cloth and lying in a manger."

*L*uke begins chapter 2, which has become our most classic of Christmas stories, with the quaint phrase "In those days." It begins in the old time, chronological time, time shaped by the "powers that be." The emperor reigns. Time is denoted by who is in power: "Quirinius was governor of Syria" (v. 2). The way people "tell time" can be a significant theological act, as Luke recognizes. So the story begins in the old time—the old age: "In those days." Even the words sound tired and hopeless.

But something happens, and the story ends on "this day" (v. 11). A new time has entered the world—a new age. "This day" is not merely a temporal notation but an eschatological affirmation; it is *kairos* time, not *chronos* time—a significant moment, not a quantifiable span of seconds or minutes. It is time shaped by the character and quality of the new event that has happened and changed the world—the birth of the Messiah. This new time is characterized not by the drudgery of business as usual or the threat of imperial power but by the in-breaking of the heavenly realm, the song of angels, and the "good news of great joy for all the people" (v. 10).

From the viewpoint of the emperor—the "powers that be"—it may even be a treasonous time. For "this day" has a political dimension; this new time is a direct challenge to the imperial world "in those days." There is a new Savior, a title formerly reserved for the emperor. There is a new Messiah, the royal, anointed one who will liberate Israel from Roman occupation. And there is a new Lord, who will inaugurate a new reign. Indeed, this new reign is signaled by its announcement to lowly shepherds rather than to those in the halls of power. A story that begins with a threatening decree of Emperor Augustus ends with the joyful, treasonous proclamation and praise of shepherds. Something odd and extraordinary has happened indeed!

With the Messiah's birth comes a time characterized not by fear but by the freedom and joy of the announcement "Do not be afraid," which is repeatedly proclaimed by the angels. "Those days" are governed by fear. The political powers, in both Jesus' day and our own, play on fear to get their way—whether it be the fear of the emperor, the fear of terrorists, the fear of the foreign "other," or the fear of death. But with "this day" comes a new possibility. The first words spoken after Jesus' birth are "'Do not be afraid; for see—I

am bringing you good news of great joy for all the people.'"
Contemporary preachers may seek to tell the story in such
a way as to move believers from the fear that grips so many
lives to the joyful "Fear not" of the angels' proclamation.

As astonishing as this change from "those days" to
"this day" is, however, the way in which the new time arrives
is even more surprising. The turning point in the story occurs
in one extremely understated verse: "And she gave birth to
her firstborn son and wrapped him in bands of cloth, and
laid him in a manger, because there was no room for them in
the inn" (2:7). Before this verse, the story is "in those days."
After this verse, "this day" has arrived. Yet the event of the
birth itself is shared with few details and little fanfare.

So many of our Christmas carols paint sentimental,
idealized pictures of Jesus' birth: "Silent night, holy night.
All is calm, all is bright"; or "How silently, how silently, the
wondrous gift is given!" Surely there was plenty of noise surrounding Jesus' birth, from the laboring mother in pain to
the squalling newborn, though such details are obviously not
important to Luke. But maybe that's not the kind of "silence"
the hymns have in mind. "In those days," Jesus' actual birth
really does not make much "noise." It is simply the unex-
ceptional birth of another child to poor parents in a small,
crowded backwater town in the empire. No one in any posi-
tion of power would have noticed. There would have been no
royal birth announcements. In this sense the birth was indeed a
"quiet" one, as the understated words of Luke's story suggest.

But that is the wild and holy mystery of the Messiah's
coming. This "quiet" birth is the pivotal moment in the
story, in our story. For afterward, the shepherds are star-
tled, and an angel proclaims, "'To you is born this day in
the city of David a Savior, who is the Messiah, the Lord.'"

Chapter 12

GLORY TO GOD

(Luke 2:13–20)

16. Accompanied Recitative

Soprano
And suddenly there was with the angel,
a multitude of the heavenly host,
praising God, and saying,

(Luke 2:13)

17. Chorus

"Glory to God in the highest,
and peace on earth,
good will towards men."

(Luke 2:14)

Luke 2:13–20

[13]And suddenly there was with the angel a multitude
of the heavenly host, praising God and saying,
[14]"Glory to God in the highest heaven,
    and on earth peace among those whom he favors!"
[15]When the angels had left them and gone into heaven,
the shepherds said to one another, "Let us go now
to Bethlehem and see this thing that has taken place,

which the Lord has made known to us." [16]So they went with haste and found Mary and Joseph, and the child lying in the manger. [17]When they saw this, they made known what had been told them about this child; [18]and all who heard it were amazed at what the shepherds told them. [19]But Mary treasured all these words and pondered them in her heart. [20]The shepherds returned, glorifying and praising God for all they had heard and seen, as it had been told them.

The shepherds were already terrified, or "sore afraid," as more archaic language puts it, when one angel appeared to them, announcing good news. The "great joy" of the proclamation of the Savior's birth is then multiplied through a double and intensified vision when "a multitude of the heavenly host" appeared. One imagines the sky filled with angelic beings as far into the stratosphere as the shepherds could see, worshiping with a deafening cacophony of praise, using words that epitomize the Christmas message: "'Glory to God in the highest heaven and on earth peace among those he favors!'"

The shepherds' natural response is fear. This should come as no surprise by now—Zechariah and Mary reacted this way too, as did just about anyone recorded throughout Scripture who was confronted with a heavenly being. The angels' words are always the same: "Do not be afraid."

Some Christian traditions have celebrated "fear of God" as a virtue, generally linked to contrition for our sins, and those of us who cherish a more loving and grace-filled relationship with God tend to minimize such notions. But perhaps we would all do well to recapture that sense of holy fear—not a cowering before some malevolent spirit but an awe before that which (or Whom) is far beyond our comprehension or knowledge, greater than our fragile, flawed, and mortal selves.

A capable performance of Handel's chorus of "Glory to God in the highest and peace on earth" may help us recapture that sense of awe that the shepherds felt, humbled by such a great heavenly chorus proclaiming those words.

The angels certainly know that this new child is the genuine king who has come to bring peace. In verse 14 they pronounce blessed those on whom the peace of this new king will rest. This is not the last time Luke's readers will hear that proclamation. When Jesus makes his triumphal entry into Jerusalem near the end of his mission, the crowds will echo this Christmas proclamation as they shout out that this great king brings " 'peace in heaven, and glory in the highest' " (19:38). The literary device *inclusio*, the repetition of an idea or phrase, is meant to alert readers to what the author considers to be especially important. The great humorist Mark Twain was fond of pointing out that he was born when Halley's Comet appeared in 1835, and he predicted that he would exit life when this same comet returned on its seventy-six-year cycle. True to his promise, Twain died one day after the comet made its reappearance in 1910. Readers often allude to this celestial inclusio as a testament to Twain's special place within the literary community. Luke's artful use of his inclusio helps the believer focus on a central message of this night: that Jesus is the true king who brings us lasting peace. With all that will be said and sung this Christmas Eve, Luke wants us to know that the king of peace is here.

For those who analyze biblical texts and translations, the peace the angels proclaim can invite some confusion. Is this peace only "among those whom [God] favors," as the

NRSV says, or peace "to men of good will" (*Douay-Rheims Bible*), or is it, as the KJV and Handel suggest, "peace [and] good will toward men"? Translations may always fall short of the truly awe-inspiring message originally intended, but the Greek term in question here, *eudokia*, often translated "good pleasure" (or "well-pleased-ness") consistently indicates God's grace and desire to save. The angels are not announcing that peace is at hand only for those who have pleased God or for those of goodwill to one another, but rather that the peace to be realized—the earthly counterpart of God's own heavenly glory—is God's gracious gift, bestowed at God's good pleasure. It is to this gracious God that "glory" is sung.

While Handel and many a church reading cut the passage off after the angels' great proclamation, to do so is to cut off the responses to the angelic announcement. Each response is offered as a proper model for how to react to the hearing of the gospel. The heavenly choir offers the first response in their song of glory. One response is simply to praise God. The shepherds obey the angel and announce what they heard to other people who, in turn, are amazed. Finally, at the end of the story, the shepherds glorify and praise God "for all they had heard and seen." They not only praise God but announce the good news to others. Mary offers a much quieter and more personal option. She "treasured all these words and pondered them in her heart." The good news inspires both private wonder and public celebration, both of which find favor with God.

Chapter 13
REJOICE GREATLY
(Zechariah 9:9–12)

18. Air

Soprano
Rejoice greatly, O daughter of Zion;
shout, O daughter of Jerusalem!
Behold, thy King cometh unto thee;
He is the righteous Saviour,
and He shall speak peace unto the heathen.
Rejoice greatly.

(Zech. 9:9–10)

Zechariah 9:9-12

[9]Rejoice greatly, O daughter Zion!
   Shout aloud, O daughter Jerusalem!
Lo, your king comes to you;
   triumphant and victorious is he,
humble and riding on a donkey,
   on a colt, the foal of a donkey.
[10]He will cut off the chariot from Ephraim
   and the war-horse from Jerusalem;
and the battle bow shall be cut off,
   and he shall command peace to the nations;
his dominion shall be from sea to sea,
   and from the River to the ends of the earth.

[11]As for you also, because of the blood of my covenant with you,
    I will set your prisoners free from the waterless pit.
[12]Return to your stronghold, O prisoners of hope;
    today I declare that I will restore to you double.

*T*he prophet Zechariah announces the coming of a king as
the occasion of joyful expectation for the people of Jerusalem. Christian eyes cannot help but see Jesus on that foal,
riding into Jerusalem. All four Gospels remember Zechariah's prophecy as Jesus enters the holy city and begins
his final journey to the cross. But even beyond that iconic
image, Zechariah's description of a king who comes to
bring peace to all people—even to "the heathen"—seems
to allude to a human ruler whose victorious appearance will
signal God's renewed reign.

      Who was this king Zechariah describes in chapter 9?
Was Zechariah thinking of a victorious king witnessed in
his own lifetime? Although the geographical references in
9:1–8 offer tantalizing suggestions for the itineraries of various historical figures, they are far from conclusive. Should
we think of Darius I (522–486 BCE), the Persian king who
authorized the rebuilding of the temple in Jerusalem and
who passed through Judah early in his reign to deal with a
revolt in Egypt? Do the allusions to Greece and the defeat of
Tyre point to the much later arrival of Alexander the Great
(333 BCE), who was remembered in legends as receiving
a wonderful reception in Jerusalem? Or does the passage
present a purely ideal figure, portrayed in imagery that
revives ancient motifs from Zion theology about Judah's
royal line? Whether this is a purely ideal figure or an ide-
alistic portrayal of some individual who is now difficult to

identify, we come to the same expectation: a king who will be different from the general experience of kings, both in Israel and among the empires of the world.

This king and his victorious appearance are clearly associated with the work of God. The herald's cry in verse 9, "Rejoice greatly, O daughter Zion! . . . Lo, your king comes to you," recalls earlier proclamations of the advent of God's mercy:

> Sing and rejoice, O daughter Zion! For lo, I will come and dwell in your midst, says the LORD.
> (Zech. 2:10)

> Sing aloud, O daughter Zion;
>   shout, O Israel!
> Rejoice and exult with all your heart,
>   O daughter Jerusalem!

> The king of Israel, the LORD, is in your midst;
>   a warrior who gives victory.
> (Zeph. 3:14, 15b, 17a)

Zechariah 9:9 offers a series of descriptors for this king that merit close attention. The NRSV rendering of the first pair of these as "triumphant and victorious" is easily misunderstood as applied to a king's military prowess; the Hebrew words are more literally rendered "righteous and saved." The KJV comes closer, in this case, with "he is just and having salvation," and Handel takes the declaration a step further, calling this king "a righteous Savior."

The second pair of descriptors, describing the king as "humble and riding on a donkey," portrays a monarch

not bent on destruction but coming to make peace. The
donkey is indeed a humble animal, but its real significance
lies in the fact that it is associated with the business of life
rather than the business of death. It is the animal used on
the farm to help in the production of food and in the town
to carry people and goods. It is the very antithesis of the
horse, at that time largely an animal used for war. The colt
therefore symbolizes the very acts that the messianic king
is to perform: taking away the chariots and warhorses and
breaking the battle bows. The king's arrival and the mode
of his arrival thus announce the end of war and the beginning of a universal peace under his rule.

Zechariah's final promise—a restoration of double
what was lost—can inspire us to reflect on the promise of
life in Jesus Christ. It is in Jesus that we too are restored
doubly: we are restored in life, and we are restored in death.
In Christ Jesus the promise of victory and triumph is not
only about the wars we face with the powers of this world;
we are promised victory over the ultimate enemy, death
itself. Such a victory and such a promise are not a denial of
death's reality but a promise of restoration, of wholeness.
As children of the covenant, we yoke our hearts to this
promise of life and peace over death and destruction, and
we live for its realization.

Chapter 14
THE LAME SHALL LEAP
(Isaiah 35:1–7)

19. Recitative

Alto
Then shall the eyes of the blind be opened,
and the ears of the deaf unstopped.
Then shall the lame man leap as an hart,
and the tongue of the dumb shall sing.

(Isa. 35:5–6)

Isaiah 35:1–7

¹The wilderness and the dry land shall be glad,
   the desert shall rejoice and blossom;
like the crocus ²it shall blossom abundantly,
   and rejoice with joy and singing.
The glory of Lebanon shall be given to it,
   the majesty of Carmel and Sharon.
They shall see the glory of the LORD,
   the majesty of our God.

³Strengthen the weak hands,
   and make firm the feeble knees.
⁴Say to those who are of a fearful heart,
   "Be strong, do not fear!

Here is your God.
He will come with vengeance,
with terrible recompense.
He will come and save you."

⁵Then the eyes of the blind shall be opened,
and the ears of the deaf unstopped;
⁶then the lame shall leap like a deer,
and the tongue of the speechless sing for joy.
For waters shall break forth in the wilderness,
and streams in the desert;
⁷the burning sand shall become a pool,
and the thirsty ground springs of water;
the haunt of jackals shall become a swamp,
the grass shall become reeds and rushes.

We are accustomed to read in sacred Scriptures that the people of God are to rejoice—even to "rejoice greatly," as Zechariah reminds us. Many a psalm makes this point. But in this chapter, as the prophet shares God's vision for Judah, even the desert—the dry places and the wilderness— is seen rejoicing in God's glory. The created order shares in the divine glory and in the work of reconciliation: "The wilderness and the dry land shall be glad, the desert shall rejoice and blossom; like the crocus it shall blossom abundantly, and rejoice with joy and singing" (vv. 1–2). A land that was scorched by the enemy in war will be renewed and restored as the people are reminded that they and the land belong to God. God's grace extends not only to all humanity but to all of creation.

Reading this passage during Advent, we are reminded that with the Messiah's coming, judgment makes room for salvation. God's graciousness and generosity are expressed to all of creation. God has not given up on God's original purpose for creation; the intrusions and breaks that are caused by sin are met with God's judgment as the way is prepared for salvation. The God of creation is faithful and will bring all things to their rightful end.

If Isaiah's prophecy imagines God's reach beyond humanity on to all creation, humanity can also take heart that it is included in God's care for all creation. The good news at Advent is that God has not taken off on a retreat. The God who cares for the dry and barren places cares for each and all of us. God shows up even in the desert and barren places of life to await us with renewal, restoration, and salvation. The God who cares for the earth also cares for us, offering change not only for the wild and barren places but also for those who are faint in heart and weak at the knees. According to the prophet, "weak hands and feeble knees" are to be strengthened. In anticipation of the God who awaits us in a new future, we are challenged "to be strong and of good courage."

The circumstances on the ground that confront God's people on a daily basis are similar to the desert and the wilderness, but the God who awaits us is faithful and has prepared a new future for the covenant people. Hope includes a new confidence that the barren and dry places will be made verdant. The presence of God provides courage and strength for all who are timid and afraid of tomorrow.

There are rational and genuine reasons why the people of Judah, Isaiah's audience, were scared. Enemies are real and powerful. In their own strength and efforts, the people would be made like the dry places and barren land, but the God who has covenanted to restore creation

is faithful and will come to save them. It is the promise of
divine presence that strengthens sinking hands and failing
knees. From a physical point of view, Judah is no match
for Assyria; but all creation, including the dry and barren
places, can give glory to God because God is on the way to
save God's people. "Behold, your God is coming" in liberation and salvation.

The divine presence means deliverance from sin,
separation, and all its consequences. The prophet points to
the marks of salvation in the new future that awaits God's
people. "Then the eyes of the blind shall be opened, and
the ears of the deaf unstopped; then the lame shall leap like
a deer; and the tongue of the speechless sing for joy" (vv.
5–6). The healing of those with physical disabilities is a
messianic sign. It is a sign of the time of salvation ushered
in by the one who is expected. Jesus witnesses to this when
John the Baptist sends to ask if he is the expected one: " 'Go
and tell John what you hear and see: the blind receive their
sight, the lame walk, the lepers are cleansed, the deaf hear,
the dead are raised, the poor have good news brought to
them' " (Matt. 11:4–5).

The restoration of health and agency revives all people for a new age marked by God's peace and salvation.
All—the most vulnerable, the most resigned, those most in
the grip of despair and death—are summoned to newness.

Chapter 15
HE SHALL FEED HIS FLOCK
(Isaiah 40:10–11)

20. Duet (Part 1)

(Alto &) Soprano
He shall feed His flock like a shepherd;
and He shall gather the lambs with His arm,
and carry them in His bosom, and gently lead
those that are with young.

(Isa. 40:11)

Isaiah 40:10-11

¹⁰See, the Lord G od comes with might,
and his arm rules for him;
his reward is with him,
and his recompense before him.
¹¹He will feed his flock like a shepherd;
he will gather the lambs in his arms,
and carry them in his bosom,
and gently lead the mother sheep.

*H*andel draws heavily on the early verses of Isaiah 40, the beginning of those chapters called Second Isaiah (chapters 40–55). Movements 2–4 of *Messiah* encompass Isaiah

40:1–5 with proclamations of comfort, images of valleys raised and mountains made low, and promises of glory so magnificent that all the earth will see it. Four movements later, the librettist jumps to verse 9, where God's herald receives her instruction: "Say to the cities of Judah, 'Here is your God.'"

Now, after words from First Isaiah, the Gospel of Luke, and Zechariah, we return to Isaiah 40:9-10 to read a description of this God the herald will tell us to behold. Isaiah draws emphatic attention to the content of the herald's message. Three times he repeats the attention-grabbing word "Behold," more colloquially translated "Look," or "See" in NRSV. The three calls to see build on one another:

> "See, your God!"
> See, your GOD comes with might   . . .
> See, your God's reward is with him,
>   and his recompense before him.

In sharp contrast to the interpretation of the Babylonian disaster presented by other prophets (e.g., Jeremiah, Ezekiel, and even First Isaiah), who accuse the people of causing the catastrophe by rampant sinfulness, Second Isaiah puts aside blaming and accusing speech, replaces punishments with rewards, and shows the people a God they can trust when everything else seems to have fallen away. Isaiah creates a theological terra firma for a fearful people not in the destroyed temple, the collapsed monarchy, or the broken covenant of the past, but in God's never-failing word. At a time when other tangible and intangible ways of relating to God have collapsed, the prophetic word is their anchor. This may be why a vocabulary of speaking and calling, voice and word, and calling and commanding dominate the text. Though everything else fails, God's word endures forever, and that God comes to lead them home.

The God proclaimed by Second Isaiah comes in strength with mighty arms stretched out in triumph. But this strength itself is paradoxical, because it is not the strength of a bloody avenger, a violent brute, or a demanding judge. No, this God's strength appears in the barely thinkable power of gentleness, in tender and caring presence, in intimacy such as a shepherd expresses when gathering the wounded, scattered flock. This God draws together the scattered lambs of Judah and rebuilds Zion. This God speaks with them in this fertile, life-producing word that, once spoken, accomplishes that for which it is sent.

The juxtaposition of God's mighty arm and gentle guidance may seem to conflict, and indeed many people draw distinctions between God's metaphysical attributes—God's power, omnipotence, and so forth—and God's relational attributes—God's love and care for the world—as if they are unrelated or somehow opposed to one another. This distinction is especially concerning when we imagine God's ultimate righteousness as in conflict with God's grace, when we suggest that God's justice cannot tolerate our imperfection, as if God is not free to reconcile those he loves without the cross as a legal transaction. On the contrary, it is clear that a shepherd as strong and compassionate as the one Second Isaiah describes uses his power to guide and care for the sheep, not to scatter and punish.

Theologian Karl Barth described God in terms of God's freedom and God's love, but Barth insisted that the two must be understood dialectically; that is, the one entails the other. God's freedom is always loving, and God's love is always uncoerced and free. In the language of Second Isaiah, God's mighty arm is not that of an arbitrary tyrant but that of a gentle shepherd who nestles the flock in a motherly bosom. God's gentle nurture is indeed mighty, and God's might is gentle and nurturing. This is no ordinary shepherd.

The God we shall see, says Second Isaiah, comes with might and gentleness—two attributes that do not negate each other but rather enrich and empower each other. Both are pastoral words to a people whose long exile has found them questioning both God's power and God's love. "Here is your God!" the herald shouts to those who live in fear and uncertainty. Here is a God who is mighty to save and can be trusted to do so.

Chapter 16
HIS YOKE IS EASY
(Matthew 11:16–30)

20. Duet (Part 2)

(Alto &) Soprano
Come unto Him, all ye that labour,
come unto Him that are heavy laden,
and He will give you rest.
Take his yoke upon you, and learn of Him,
for He is meek and lowly of heart,
and ye shall find rest unto your souls.

                                    (Matt. 11:28–29)

21. Chorus

His yoke is easy, and His burthen is light.

                                    (Matt. 11:30)

Matthew 11:16–19, 25–30

[16]"But to what will I compare this generation? It is like children sitting in the marketplaces and calling to one another,
[17]'We played the flute for you, and you did not dance; we wailed, and you did not mourn.'
[18]For John came neither eating nor drinking, and they say, 'He has a demon'; [19]the Son of Man came eating

and drinking, and they say, 'Look, a glutton and a drunkard, a friend of tax collectors and sinners!' Yet wisdom is vindicated by her deeds.". . .

[25]At that time Jesus said, "I thank you, Father, Lord of heaven and earth, because you have hidden these things from the wise and the intelligent and have revealed them to infants; [26] yes, Father, for such was your gracious will. [27]All things have been handed over to me by my Father; and no one knows the Son except the Father, and no one knows the Father except the Son and anyone to whom the Son chooses to reveal him.

[28]"Come to me, all you that are weary and are carrying heavy burdens, and I will give you rest. [29]Take my yoke upon you, and learn from me; for I am gentle and humble in heart, and you will find rest for your souls. [30]For my yoke is easy, and my burden is light."

*L*est we forget that the mighty shepherd-God whom Isaiah invites us to behold comes to earth as a humble and frequently misunderstood messiah, Handel closes part 1 of his oratorio with words from the Gospel of Matthew. Here, Jesus—like his Father God—offers comfort alongside reminders of our own weakness in light of God's unattainable glory.

"My yoke is easy, and my burden is light," Jesus says. This familiar saying, put into third person by Handel, is widely understood to mean that following Jesus is easy, because, unlike the Pharisees, Jesus is not too particular about following rules to the T. Unlike John, the bug-eating wilderness prophet, Jesus is known to love a good meal with all kinds of company and can even be persuaded to invoke the power of God to keep the wine flowing at a wedding reception. Jesus certainly presents a joie de vivre that other religious leaders do not.

However, this antinomian take on Jesus does not stand up to a close reading of the Sermon on the Mount, which expounds a more, not less, rigorous theological ethic (Matt. 5:17–20). The "easy yoke" Jesus promises is all the more perplexing in light of the strenuous demands placed on disciples in chapter 10 and the rejection depicted in chapter 11. How can Jesus offer rest when he asks so much?

What Jesus offers is not freedom from work but freedom from onerous labor. Soul-sick weariness is not the inevitable consequence of all work but rather of work to which we are ill suited, of work extracted under compulsion and motivated by fear, or of work performed in the face of futility. There is also the weariness that comes from having nothing at all to do that truly matters. The easy yoke means work that is motivated by a passionate desire to see God's kingdom realized. This is not the work we are accustomed to in our world.

So much of what is best in our world comes through focused effort. From brilliant theoretical breakthroughs to life-saving medical techniques to virtuosic musical performances, such knowledge and mastery must be pursued with diligence. If you want to excel at something, get up early, concentrate hard, stay up late, and repeat, and repeat again, and again.

But there are some things—including the most important thing—that do not work that way. Knowledge of God, closeness to God, and even faithful discipleship are not just more achievements that we can reach out and take hold of by our own power. The more we grasp after God by our own wits, the less we attain. The more pressure we put on ourselves to be more and do more for God, the farther we drift from real surrender to God. As Jesus says in verses 25–27, it is as if God is hiding from those who are good at finding things in the normal way, while those who show no prowess when it comes to understanding all kinds of other things seem to be adept at receiving the gift of God's gracious self-disclosure. It is the spiritual "infants," the least theologically articulate people, those with the fewest illusions about their own powers of understanding, who know how to receive Jesus in humility and so gain access to the one he came to reveal.

Prefacing that point, Jesus tells a parable about the difference between himself and John the Baptist and the rejection they have in common. He compares the people to fickle children who keep changing the rules of the game. John came "neither eating nor drinking" (v. 18), and they did not care for his style at all. He was too old-school for their taste—too stern and demanding. So they played the flute and said, "Come on, John, lighten up. Lay off the hellfire and dance to our tune." Then Jesus came and was ready to dance—dance as they had never dreamed! Every meal was a party, as long as everyone was invited. Then they wailed about the company Jesus kept and called him "glutton" and "drunkard" (v. 19).

Jesus' point here is that neither extreme feels palatable to us. Both of these messages are a threat to our hard-won autonomy. We long to set our own criteria for faithfulness, maintaining a happy medium between John's stifling demands and Jesus' frightening inclusiveness. So we keep changing our tune, insisting on the moderation (or is it the mediocrity?) that we can secure for ourselves, not the extraordinary future that God dreams for us and the world.

In short, any who believe that they are responsible for their own salvation, through military might or political power, through intellectual prowess or personal magnetism, have no need of the comforting arms of Jesus. Jesus will not trouble them with heaven's gifts. To those who recognize their need for a savior, however, Jesus comes with comfort enough, lifting life's burdens and offering rest even for the lonely soul.

PART 2

CHRIST'S PASSION AND RESURRECTION

Chapter 17

BEHOLD THE LAMB

(John 1:29–34)

22. Chorus

Behold the Lamb of God,
that taketh away the sin of the world.
(John 1:29)

John 1:29–34

[29]The next day he saw Jesus coming toward him and declared, "Here is the Lamb of God who takes away the sin of the world! [30]This is he of whom I said, 'After me comes a man who ranks ahead of me because he was before me.' [31]I myself did not know him; but I came baptizing with water for this reason, that he might be revealed to Israel." [32]And John testified, "I saw the Spirit descending from heaven like a dove, and it remained on him. [33]I myself did not know him, but the one who sent me to baptize with water said to me, 'He on whom you see the Spirit descend and remain is the one who baptizes with the Holy Spirit.' [34]And I myself have seen and have testified that this is the Son of God."

*T*eresa of Avila, a sixteenth-century Spanish mystic, is credited with saying, "Christ has no body now on earth but yours, no hands but yours, no feet but yours." The concept has taken on a popular presence in Christian spirituality and reflects a common understanding of what some call an incarnational theology—the idea that we are to be Jesus Christ to the world. At its foundation, incarnational theology reminds us all that God became incarnate—became flesh—in Jesus Christ to embody fully God's love for the world. Teresa of Avila takes this incarnational theology one step further and calls on us to incarnate Christ in our own selves and to love the world as Jesus did, even to the point of "always carrying in the body the death of Jesus, so that the life of Jesus may also be made visible in our bodies" as the apostle Paul writes to the church at Corinth (2 Cor. 4:10).

In John the Baptist, who speaks the "Behold" with which Handel begins part 2 of *Messiah*, we see a different understanding of incarnational theology. Here, John the Baptist sees Jesus, God incarnate, coming and calls attention to Jesus, testifying to all within hearing distance that he is one who baptizes with the Holy Spirit. John the Baptist plays an important role, providing testimony as to who Jesus is and pointing the way so that others come to recognize Jesus Christ.

In the 1990s, when the What Would Jesus Do? campaign was all the rage, many people wore bracelets with the letters WWJD on them. For some, it was just a fad, but ideally, the bracelets were tangible reminders that we are followers of Jesus who are to be guided by his actions in every facet of our lives. It's good to ask, "What would Jesus do?" but it may also mislead us into thinking we can really know what Jesus would do in a given situation and that if we did know, we would be capable of doing it. Lest our honorable desire to live lives that embody Christ overreach into some messianic identity that says we are Christ to the world, it may be better for us to ask, "WWJBD? What would John the Baptist do?"

To do as John the Baptist did is to call attention to Jesus Christ and then to say to all who are within hearing distance, "Hey, look! See! God is alive. God is in our midst. The Holy Spirit is at work in us and through and for us and even in spite of us! Behold! The Lamb of God!"

The image of a lamb often communicates a weak, vulnerable animal ready for sacrifice or slaughter. However, as it is used here and in some other Jewish writings, the lamb is powerful. The lamb reigns in the heavens and will bring about judgment on the wicked and secure salvation for the righteous. It is in relation to this lamb that John recognizes his own inferiority or lower rank. Jesus "ranks ahead" of John because Jesus precedes him in time (i.e., Jesus pre-existed; see John 1:1–5); because Jesus baptizes with the Spirit, and John, only with water; and finally because in God's plans John is preparatory in function (see Isa. 40:3 in John 1:23). However, John's testimony is not diminished by this. Though "no one has ever seen God" (v. 18), just various manifestations of God, John has seen the Son of God. John has seen God because God has allowed it, and now he voices the testimony—that Jesus is the Son of God—even before Jesus demonstrates it in his earthly ministry.

Though some contend that John recognized Jesus as the Messiah at first sight, it is clear from John's words that this was not the case; twice he says, "I myself did not know him" (vv. 31, 33). Rather, by seeking to follow God through his calling to baptize people with water, "so that [the Messiah] may be revealed to Israel," John is ready to see Christ and proclaim him to others. Like John the Baptist, we can watch for and call attention to Jesus, telling everyone that he is the Lamb of God who takes away the sins of the world.

Chapter 18
HE WAS DESPISED
(Isaiah 52:13–53:3)

23. Air

Alto
He was despised and rejected of men,
a man of sorrows and acquainted with grief.
(Isa. 53:3)

He gave His back to the smiters,
and His cheeks to them that plucked off His hair:
He hid not His face from shame and spitting.
(Isa. 50:6)

Isaiah 52:13–53:3

[13]See, my servant shall prosper;
    he shall be exalted and lifted up,
    and shall be very high.
[14]Just as there were many who were astonished at him
    —so marred was his appearance, beyond human
    semblance,
    and his form beyond that of mortals—
[15]so he shall startle many nations;
    kings shall shut their mouths because of him;
for that which had not been told them they shall see,

and that which they had not heard they shall
contemplate.
^{53:1}Who has believed what we have heard?
And to whom has the arm of the LORD been
revealed?
²For he grew up before him like a young plant,
and like a root out of dry ground;
he had no form or majesty that we should look at him,
nothing in his appearance that we should desire him.
³He was despised and rejected by others;
a man of suffering and acquainted with infirmity;
and as one from whom others hide their faces
he was despised, and we held him of no account.

*F*our movements of the oratorio's part 2 draw from the Servant Songs identified in Second Isaiah (parts of chapters
42, 49, 50, and 52–53) describing "my servant" in both his
humiliation and exaltation. Of the twenty occurrences of
"servant" in Second Isaiah, thirteen most clearly identify
the "servant of the LORD" with Israel. The seven remaining occurrences are in the Servant Songs, and scholars have
long debated who is meant in these passages.

The two interpretive poles have been a collective and
an individual interpretation. The figure could represent
Israel, as a king embodies his people or as conceived in the
concept of "corporate personality." But since the Servant
here has a mission to Israel, this personification could refer
to a king or a prophet. Many biblical figures, such as Moses,
a prophet, King Cyrus of Persia, or the writer of Second
Isaiah, have been suggested. If the Servant is an individual,
is he historical or someone still to come? By heightening
the individualization of the figure, is the writer looking for

one who would come to embody more fully who the Lord's
Servant should be? Traditionally, the church has seen the
Servant of this passage as fulfilled in Jesus Christ.

The Servant Song from which Handel draws begins
by describing the servant as "so marred was his appearance, beyond human semblance, and his form beyond
that of mortals" (52:14), and for this disfigurement, he is
"despised and rejected" (53:3).

These are the people in our own day who are
despised and rejected, those from whom others hide their
faces, those whom the world holds to be of no account. We
have learned to ignore the homeless woman who mutters
obscenities on the sidewalk. We read the newspaper dis-
passionately about desperate refugees herded into a border
camp to await deportation. We assume the worst when we
meet black teenagers with sweatshirt hoods hiding their
faces. We are upset when we see journalists' photos of Iraqi
citizens held and tortured in our prison cells, but we soon
move on to something else. We hear—but cannot remember—unfathomable statistics about the numbers of people
murdered in our city, or afflicted with HIV, or orphaned in
Africa, or dying of hunger on arid fields.

Isaiah's community assumes that these rejected,
shamed, ignored people, this Suffering Servant or servants,
were guilty of some crime and were, therefore, to blame
for their own plight. "Struck down by God," their trouble
must be of their own doing. Even today, we might agree
that those who suffer often do so by the acts of their own
hands, by refusing to take responsibility for their lives.
Even if we summon a more compassionate perspective, we
can easily become numb to their dilemma, anesthetized by
the persistent onslaught of violent images buffeting us. It's
too much to take in, so we allow the suffering of others to

brush by us until it ceases to disturb us. We are outraged at injustice less frequently. We become jaded and cynical.

As we look away, Isaiah reminds us that this Suffering Servant is the very one to whom God turns God's own attention. God does not turn away. Isaiah's song offers reassurance and hope for anyone who is downtrodden. The rejected, the afflicted are the apple of God's eye. The ones the world looks down on, God lifts up. Those who have been dismissed by everybody else are the ones God "exalts."

It is telling that the Suffering Servant in the text is silent. He offers no protest or defense when he is rejected, and he makes no plea for attention or help. The poem speaks of his life and death, but it never invites or allows him to speak of his own experience. How often is it still true today that those whom the world counts for nothing never get to find their own voices? Do we not hear their suffering because we have turned a deaf ear? Or is it because we have never made it safe for them to tell us the truth about their lives?

During Advent, when we anticipate the coming of one whose birth would be undignified and whose death would be despicable, let us look at those despised, rejected people and see people that God loves—perhaps even people on whom God's spirit rests.

Chapter 19
HE BORE OUR GRIEFS
(Isaiah 53:4–5, 9–12)

24. Chorus

Surely He hath borne our griefs,
and carried our sorrows!
He was wounded for our transgressions,
He was bruised for our iniquities;
the chastisement of our peace was upon Him.

(Isa. 53:4–5)

25. Chorus

And with his stripes we are healed.

(Isa. 53:5)

Isaiah 53:4–5, 9–12

[4]Surely he has borne our infirmities
     and carried our diseases;
yet we accounted him stricken,
     struck down by God, and afflicted.
[5]But he was wounded for our transgressions,
     crushed for our iniquities;
upon him was the punishment that made us whole,
     and by his bruises we are healed.

.   .   .   .

⁹They made his grave with the wicked
and his tomb with the rich,
although he had done no violence,
and there was no deceit in his mouth.

¹⁰Yet it was the will of the LORD to crush
him with pain.
When you make his life an offering for sin,
he shall see his offspring, and shall prolong
his days;
through him the will of the LORD shall prosper.
¹¹Out of his anguish he shall see light;
he shall find satisfaction through his knowledge.
The righteous one, my servant, shall make
many righteous,
and he shall bear their iniquities.
¹²Therefore I will allot him a portion with the great,
and he shall divide the spoil with the strong;
because he poured out himself to death,
and was numbered with the transgressors;
yet he bore the sin of many,
and made intercession for the transgressors.

*F*or Christian theology, this segment of the fourth Suffering Servant song in Isaiah 53 constitutes one of the central scriptural passages for reflection on redemptive suffering. Because early Christians (Acts 8:32–35) identified the Suffering Servant with Jesus, this description of one who "was wounded for our transgressions" (Isa. 53:5) has become part of the Christian passion narrative. As such, this text provides fertile ground for exploring some crucial and complex questions related to God's redemptive work through Jesus' suffering.

We must begin by acknowledging that redemptive suffering is a dangerous idea. The idea that God redeems through suffering is used to justify abuse or to put a pious gloss on passivity in the face of human pain. It also becomes entangled in forms of internalized oppression that keep someone from resisting his or her own maltreatment. Because of these dangers, many Christians emphasize the redemptive nature of Christ's life and ministry more so than the redemptive nature of his suffering. However, these verses force us to reckon with the idea that an innocent man's torment may be the way God chooses to bring restoration.

These verses make clear that the Suffering Servant's affliction is not God's judgment upon him, as might be assumed from earlier verses. Rather, the speaker realizes that this innocent man is "crushed for our iniquities." The onlookers are not witnessing a case of just deserts but rather an act of vicarious suffering for their own redemption. The "LORD has laid on him the iniquity of us all" (53:6). The translation in the Common English Bible is even more powerful: "But the LORD let fall on him all our crimes."

We may find verse 10 the most troubling of all: "Yet it was the will of the LORD to crush him with pain." The text moves quickly to identify God's purpose. Indeed, some translations refuse the full stop: "But the LORD chose to crush him by disease, That, if he made himself an offering for guilt, He might see offspring and have long life, And that through him the LORD's purpose might prosper" (JPS). God's will to "crush him and make him suffer" (CEB) is not for the sake of causing him pain but for the sake of redemption. Through his suffering, the Servant is exalted. By his suffering, the Servant makes "intercession for the transgressors" (v. 12). This man's affliction and torment are part of God's plan for restoration and wholeness.

What does it mean that God chooses to use a man's affliction and torment as the means to redemption? Key to this reflection is clarity about the relationship between God and the Suffering Servant. We meet the Suffering Servant in Isaiah 42:1 with the announcement "Here is my servant, whom I uphold, my chosen, in whom my soul delights; I have put my spirit upon him; he will bring forth justice to the nations. In Isaiah 50:4–9, the Servant recognizes the torment that awaits him, pledges his faithfulness to God, and asserts that God will vindicate him. There are still a number of troubling theological elements here, but involuntary suffering is not one of them. Taken as a whole, the Suffering Servant narrative depicts one who willingly takes on suffering as an act of faith in a God who remains present and will redeem. The Servant gives himself to God, volunteering his body as an instrument for God's redemptive work.

The Servant's chosen status and willful participation make plain that any application of Suffering Servant imagery to involuntary suffering is utterly inappropriate. By contrast, an appropriate analogy is the action of a nonviolent activist who willingly subjects him- or herself to the brutality of an opponent in order to expose the brutality of an oppressor: God works through these beaten bodies to change hearts and minds, to establish justice, and to restore community.

This passage can open our eyes to God's redemptive work in social contexts where people mistreat one another. God does not step in to rescue the one who has chosen to subject himself or herself to brutality. God does, however, vindicate this person, and this vindication serves as judgment on those who perpetrated the mistreatment. "We," the perpetrators and the onlookers, are met simultaneously with divine judgment and unearned forgiveness. In such a frame, the Suffering Servant of Isaiah 53:4–12 reminds Christians of more than our redemption through the suffering of Christ. It also alerts us to the ongoing nature of God's redemptive work as we live out our lives in the crucible of judgment and mercy.

Chapter 20

ALL WE LIKE SHEEP
(Isaiah 53:6)

26. Chorus

All we like sheep have gone astray;
we have turned every one to his own way.
And the Lord hath laid on Him the iniquity of us all.

(Isa. 53:6)

> **Isaiah 53:6**
>
> ⁶All we like sheep have gone astray;
>   we have all turned to our own way,
>   and the Lord has laid on him
>   the iniquity of us all.

*T*his chorus may be the lightest movement of the four that explore Isaiah's Suffering Servant, but the energy of its melody should not blind us to the weight of its words. So complete is the common conflation of Isaiah's and Jesus' stories by Handel and by generations of Christians before and after that we do not often pause to consider what the Suffering Servant meant to its original audience. There is a certain humility and caution that this text begs of us if we are to allow it to speak on its own terms.

Isaiah's depiction of the Suffering Servant is rooted in the ancient and widespread practice of scapegoating, allowing the more widely deserved punishment for sin to fall on a single victim: "the LORD has laid on him the iniquity of us all." In the practice of ancient Israel, the high priest laid hands on a sacrificial goat, transferring the sins of Israel onto the animal, which was then slaughtered. The ritual of sacrifice demonstrated both the people's awareness of their shortcomings and God's mercy in accepting the gift of the scapegoat.

In Isaiah's prophetic imaginings, it is ultimately the whole nation of Israel that becomes the scapegoat, called to suffer—and perhaps even die—on behalf of the other nations. And slaughter has often been the price Israel has been forced to pay over the past several millennia. Modern survivors of the Holocaust have agonized for several generations over whether that deadly atrocity represented a breathtakingly high-priced servanthood or simply the most horrific victimhood ever and another nail in God's coffin.

It is volition and the spawning of redemptive energies that set the Suffering Servant apart from other scapegoats who are simply involuntary victims. Within the Christian tradition the picture of the Servant's volition finds poignant reexpression in Jesus' words in John: " 'No one has greater love than this, to lay down one's life for one's friends' " (John 15:13). This type of sacrificial suffering, instead of being only a dead end for the victim and life as usual for the wider community, opens the way for a redemption that ultimately subsumes all creation.

Out of context, the term "suffering servant" may have no sense of redemption for those who hear it. In this text, however, the Suffering Servant guides the faithful to God's redemption. Isaiah's vision of the Suffering Servant and its historical origins lead us to ask both, "Who are today's sacrificial victims bearing the cost for ways we have gone astray?" and "How shall we live out our suffering servanthood?" We are both sinners and participants in the redemption of a sinful world.

There are voluntary servants in our world—nurses, teachers, utility workers—who work long, hard hours to help the rest of us. Some, like social workers, firefighters, and police, work to remedy problems caused by the mistakes and misbehaviors of others. But who are those that involuntarily suffer for the failings of the rest of society? Scapegoating may be virtually obsolete as a religious practice, but it is alive and well nearly everywhere else. Immigrants, refugees, various minorities, the young, the elderly, the poor, and the infirm all get burdened with the reluctance of others to shoulder responsibility for the problems that afflict us all. Many millions die each year owing to the willingness of some to allow others to suffer so that they can maintain relatively affluent styles of living. Affluent cultures send their poor to prison to avoid questions of cultural injustice or to war to fight and die on their behalf. Our sin is well-described as "going astray" and "choosing our own way," for it is often the outshoot of privileging our own desires over the common good.

In considering our own opportunities for service, we must be careful not to overspiritualize or idealize the Suffering Servant, thus obscuring the need for change and justifying less just and critical local and global citizenship. Considering the Suffering Servant as a proper model for Christian discipleship may lead us to explore God's dynamic, saving activity through the work of servants who are willing to sacrifice and suffer on behalf of others whose lives are marked by involuntary suffering. All of us aspiring disciples, who vacillate between wandering astray and seeking to follow the Way, need this reminder of the ultimate sacrifice borne by God's own flesh and this challenge to live out our own suffering servanthood on behalf of the redemption of all of God's creation.

Chapter 21
THEY LAUGH HIM TO SCORN
(Psalm 22:1–15)

27. Accompanied Recitative

Tenor
All they that see Him laugh Him to scorn;
they shoot out their lips,
and shake their heads, saying:

(Ps. 22:7)

28. Chorus

"He trusted in God that He would deliver Him;
let Him deliver him, if He delight in Him."

(Ps. 22:8)

Psalm 22:1–15

¹My God, my God, why have you forsaken me?
Why are you so far from helping me, from
the words of my groaning?
²O my God, I cry by day, but you do not answer;
and by night, but find no rest.

³Yet you are holy,
enthroned on the praises of Israel.
⁴In you our ancestors trusted;
they trusted, and you delivered them.

[5]To you they cried, and were saved;
   in you they trusted, and were not put to shame.

[6]But I am a worm, and not human;
   scorned by others, and despised by the people.
[7]All who see me mock at me;
   they make mouths at me, they shake their heads;
[8]"Commit your cause to the LORD; let him deliver—
   let him rescue the one in whom he delights!"

[9]Yet it was you who took me from the womb;
   you kept me safe on my mother's breast.
[10]On you I was cast from my birth,
   and since my mother bore me you have been
      my God.
[11]Do not be far from me,
   for trouble is near
   and there is no one to help.

[12]Many bulls encircle me,
   strong bulls of Bashan surround me;
[13]they open wide their mouths at me,
   like a ravening and roaring lion.

[14]I am poured out like water,
   and all my bones are out of joint;
my heart is like wax;
   it is melted within my breast;
[15]my mouth is dried up like a potsherd,
   and my tongue sticks to my jaws;
   you lay me in the dust of death.

*P*salm 22 reads like a verbal tennis match between the conflicting emotions of an anguished believer:

Voice 1: "God, where are you?"

Voice 2: "You are the best!"

Voice 1: "Why don't you answer me?"

Voice 2: "You've been faithful to me since the day I was born!"

Voice 1: "How could you let this happen to me?"

Voice 2: "I am so grateful for your steadfast love."

The writer's back-and-forth proclamations of devotion and despair swing from one end of the arc of the pendulum of faith to the other, and his agony is visible for all the world to see. One's cries to God become all the more empty and wounding when the sole answer is that of one's tormenters, not only mocking the cries for assistance but in effect mocking the integrity and capacities of the God with whom one is in prayerful relationship: "You were so certain of God's love! Where is your God now?" The shame of being abandoned by God in a way that everyone else can see rubs salt into the raw and bleeding gashes of the psalmist's wounded spirit. If this is how God treats God's friends, then who needs enemies?

The dilemma is compounded by the fact that the psalmist is a person of deep faith. Despite his feelings of desolation, he nonetheless refers to God as "my God." Not "O God," or even just "God," but "my God." The pure and abiding trust that the writer has in God conveys his despair at being abandoned by the One who elicits that faith. God, who once seemed as close and life-giving as the person's own breath, is now distant and removed. The one who has felt the security of God's proximity feels even more keenly the shattering devastation of the Almighty's presumed absence.

It is not surprising that Jesus prayed using the words of the Twenty-second Psalm. As one whose limbs really were wrenched out of joint (v. 14), where passersby mocked and enemies snorted (vv. 7, 12), he did what any faithful Jew might have done: prayed for deliverance with the words of Psalm 22. It makes many a faithful Christian ask how the One whom we claim is the Son of God, and so God himself, can be abandoned by God.

The psalmist's faith and Christ's oneness with God do not belie the despondency those in peril feel but rather prove that one's personal connection with God is not eradicated even by the most agonizing despair. God continues to be "my God." The psalmist questions the absence of God while at the same time affirming the divine presence. There is never any doubt that God exists, even when God's seeming abandonment brings desperation and ridicule. The person of faith may question and call on God for answers, but this very questioning implies that life is still to be found in the divine-human encounter. Faith is greater than that which seeks to destroy it.

Personal suffering certainly has the potential to cause the sufferer to withdraw into an abyss of self-pity. We pull away from God and from other people, tangled in a net of fear and anger at what we perceive as an unjust sentence that we do not deserve. Yet suffering can also have the opposite effect of drawing us into an awareness of and connection with the suffering of others. The heart of the mother who grieves over the death of her child is bound to the hearts of all the mothers who have ever buried a daughter or a son. The victim of a violent crime reads the newspaper with a keener eye to the plight of the other innocents whose lives are changed forever in an instant. The employee whose job is "downsized" has a new sensitivity to those who have lost their jobs through no fault of their own. Shared suffering connects us to a larger world at the very time we are most at risk of feeling isolated and alone. We are able to tap into the hope for healing and resurrection that resides in the life of that community.

That hope for healing and resurrection comes from the One in whom the community of faith is born in the first place: Jesus Christ. The suffering of Jesus is the suffering of God at the brokenness of the world. It thus gives context to our own suffering. Yes, the world—and life—is often painful and difficult, but our suffering is neither caused nor ignored by God. Jesus' cry to God from the cross, "My God, my God, why have you forsaken me?" simultaneously expresses both human despair and confidence in God's faithfulness to share our sorrows, hold us close, and ultimately deliver us from the clutches of death.

Chapter 22

THERE WAS NO ONE TO COMFORT HIM

(Psalm 69:7–20)

29. Accompanied Recitative

Tenor
Thy rebuke hath broken His heart:
He is full of heaviness.
He looked for some to have pity on Him,
but there was no man, neither found He
any to comfort him.

(Ps. 69:20)

Psalm 69:7–20

⁷It is for your sake that I have borne reproach,
   that shame has covered my face.
⁸I have become a stranger to my kindred,
   an alien to my mother's children.

⁹It is zeal for your house that has consumed me;
   the insults of those who insult you have fallen
      on me.
¹⁰When I humbled my soul with fasting,
   they insulted me for doing so.
¹¹When I made sackcloth my clothing,
   I became a byword to them.

[12]I am the subject of gossip for those who
    sit in the gate,
    and the drunkards make songs about me.

[13]But as for me, my prayer is to you, O Lord.
    At an acceptable time, O God,
    in the abundance of your steadfast love,
      answer me.
With your faithful help [14]rescue me
    from sinking in the mire;
let me be delivered from my enemies
    and from the deep waters.
[15]Do not let the flood sweep over me,
    or the deep swallow me up,
    or the Pit close its mouth over me.

[16]Answer me, O Lord, for your steadfast love is good;
    according to your abundant mercy, turn to me.
[17]Do not hide your face from your servant,
    for I am in distress—make haste to answer me.
[18]Draw near to me, redeem me,
    set me free because of my enemies.

[19]You know the insults I receive,
    and my shame and dishonor;
    my foes are all known to you.
[20]Insults have broken my heart,
    so that I am in despair.
I looked for pity, but there was none;
    and for comforters, but I found none.

Just as Psalm 22 speaks to Jesus' anguish on the cross, this psalm speaks to the alienation with which humankind struggles in its relationship with God. The psalmist, like Jesus, is rejected, persecuted, mocked, and insulted—not because he has forgotten God but because of his deep faithfulness.

While Psalm 69 is one of many attributed to David (thus linking it to the kingship of David and connecting Jesus to that line), it is also possible that the psalm was written at the time of the exile. This gives us two options for interpretation: as an individual lament addressed to God or as a collective cry for help. Either way, the psalm gives voice to the human who seeks God and rails at God's absence; it appeals to God for justice and requests that all who seek God's justice remember God's preferential option for the poor.

This portion of Psalm 69 comes from someone who is completely miserable. Not surprisingly, these verses have been connected to some of the "Woe is me" passages that we find in Job (e.g., Job 3), as well as to the passion narratives at the end of Jesus' life and ministry, to which Handel is building in part 2 of *Messiah*. In the later verses of the psalm text, there is an allusion to heaven and earth's praising God and to God's saving the covenant people—verses that have been linked to the joy and new life of the resurrection.

This psalm is the prayer of one who is "despised and rejected." Like Jesus and the psalmist, one can sometimes live as a stranger within one's own community. With that comes alienation from those we know and love, due not only to important issues but also to matters that sometimes seem pointless as we seek to live an authentic life, true to ourselves and true to what God has called and created us to be. Psalm 69 is a prayer for help when one is rejected by one's own family and community, when one is feeling like the stranger or the alien, for doing nothing more than seeking to do what God has called us to do or to be.

The mockery the psalmist expresses is painful to read. "I am the subject of gossip for those who sit in the gate, and the drunkards make songs about me," he says, presenting himself as an outcast among outcasts, one so lowly that even beggars and drunks reject him. Verse 20, turned from first to third person in the oratorio, laments, "Insults have broken my heart, so that I am in despair. I looked for pity, but there was none; and for comforters, but I found none."

The psalmist rails at God for God's neglect but in moments of clarity affirms God's concern and provision. The psalmist is reminded that all will occur in "an acceptable time" (v. 13) or in the fullness of time. Just when we feel the most underwater, we are reminded that God works in God's own time. In those moments when we want a sign from God but we do not get what we expect, we often assume that God has left us.

Like the psalmist, we operate a bit like the farmer in the flood who ignored two boats and a helicopter as he waited for God to lift him off his roof. We pray for God to act or speak to us, sometimes not noticing the ways God is already acting and speaking. Sometimes those revelations or epiphanies of God come in ways that we do not expect, and we are blessed when we pay attention to them. Even Job, who like the psalmist was persecuted for his faith, rails at God about all he has done in God's name. God responds to him by saying, "'Where were you when I laid the foundation of the earth?'" (Job 38:4). Where were you when all this came into being? Where were you when I created all that is?

The psalmist reminds us that on those days when life has hit us hard, we are not alone. People have been railing and angry at God throughout history, and God can take our anger. On those days when we feel far away from God, we are reminded that we are not alone, and God can take our distance. When we feel that all around us have turned their backs, the psalmist reminds us that God calls us to live into what is right in front of us. This is all God asks.

Chapter 23

SORROW LIKE UNTO HIS SORROW

(Lamentations 1:1–12)

30. Arioso

Tenor
Behold, and see if there be any sorrow
like unto His sorrow.

(Lam. 1:12)

Lamentations 1:1–12

[1]How lonely sits the city
  that once was full of people!
How like a widow she has become,
  she that was great among the nations!
She that was a princess among the provinces
  has become a vassal.

[2]She weeps bitterly in the night,
  with tears on her cheeks;
among all her lovers
  she has no one to comfort her;
all her friends have dealt treacherously with her,
  they have become her enemies.

[3]Judah has gone into exile with suffering
  and hard servitude;

she lives now among the nations,
    and finds no resting place;
her pursuers have all overtaken her
    in the midst of her distress.

[4]The roads to Zion mourn,
    for no one comes to the festivals;
all her gates are desolate,
    her priests groan;
her young girls grieve,
    and her lot is bitter.

[5]Her foes have become the masters,
    her enemies prosper,
because the Lord has made her suffer
    for the multitude of her transgressions;
her children have gone away,
    captives before the foe.

[6]From daughter Zion has departed
    all her majesty.
Her princes have become like stags
    that find no pasture;
they fled without strength
    before the pursuer.

[7]Jerusalem remembers,
    in the days of her affliction and wandering,
all the precious things
    that were hers in days of old.
When her people fell into the hand of the foe,
    and there was no one to help her,
the foe looked on mocking
    over her downfall.

⁸Jerusalem sinned grievously,
    so she has become a mockery;
all who honored her despise her,
    for they have seen her nakedness;
she herself groans,
    and turns her face away.

⁹Her uncleanness was in her skirts;
    she took no thought of her future;
her downfall was appalling,
    with none to comfort her.
"O Lord, look at my affliction,
    for the enemy has triumphed!"

¹⁰Enemies have stretched out their hands
    over all her precious things;
she has even seen the nations
    invade her sanctuary,
those whom you forbade
    to enter your congregation.

¹¹All her people groan
    as they search for bread;
they trade their treasures for food
    to revive their strength.
Look, O Lord, and see
    how worthless I have become.

¹²Is it nothing to you, all you who pass by?
    Look and see
if there is any sorrow like my sorrow,
    which was brought upon me,
which the Lord inflicted
    on the day of his fierce anger.

Lamentations was penned in the wake of the destruction of Jerusalem by the Babylonians in 586 BCE. Many people were killed in the eighteen-month siege of the city, and the lives of survivors were broken and shattered. Lamentations gives voice to those who survived this devastating experience; it is survivors' literature. In more modern terms, post-traumatic stress syndrome was a common reality for those who lived through this horrendous time. The book, traditionally thought to be written by the prophet Jeremiah, is authored by a survivor remaining in the land, seeking to address such issues.

Theologies of hope, psalms of praise, and elations of joy are silenced or, at best, reduced to faint whispers in the face of the abject devastation and unthinkable suffering of sixth-century Judah. The same holds true for the crises we endure (or at the very least, witness) today. Shootings, bombings, tragic accidents, natural disasters—what can be said in the wake of such destruction? How can it be said? Words seem frail, gratuitous, or utterly useless.

Radical suffering initially muffles the usefulness of any rational discourse. As we learn from Job and his friends, not speaking may be the most speakable thing to do. Mumbling half-hearted clichés will not help. When it is time to speak, we should not rush to comfort. Lamentations gives no vision of future restoration; no all-too-easy focus on "the next life" is allowed to obscure the painful present and the lives so filled with anguish. Consider the form of proclamation in our text: emotive poetry embedded with vivid, horrible images.

To come to terms with such suffering, the poet recalls as vividly as possible what the community has been through. Images from Israel's slavery in Egypt pervade the book and help give depth to the depiction of distress (e.g.,

1:3). Lamentations brings those suffering voices to the surface in lyrical poetry and enables the readers to relive those
moments in all of their horrific detail. That the author uses
the genre of the lament (addressed to God, vv. 11, 20),
so common in the Psalter, to convey these dreadful expe-
riences both signals the gravity of the remembrances and
constitutes an invitation to readers to join in these liturgical
moments.

The images for the city/woman are remarkable in
their range and intensity, lifting up especially the difference
between then and now. How lovely she once was! How
horrifying she now is! She is imaged as a lonely widow who
has lost her husband and as a princess from the royal pal-
ace who has become a vassal, subjected to others' whims
and wishes. She weeps bitterly, with tears flowing down
her cheeks, and she has no lovers left to comfort her, as all
her friends and allies have become her enemies. She has
been exiled, without a home of her own, enslaved to others,
and has become a victim of every pursuer, unable to offer
any resistance. She is deserted by former visitors and sup-
porters, groaning, alone, and bitter; her children have been
taken captive by enemies, who now prosper. Her honor
and strength have vanished, and her leaders have fled without resources.

And then she cries, "O LORD, look at my affliction" (v. 9). "Look, O LORD, and see how worthless I have
become" (v. 11). Even more, she cries, "All you who pass
by [readers, from every generation], look and see if there is
any sorrow like my sorrow" (v. 12).

Though the historical context for Lamentations is
clear, Handel's application of verse 12 to Christ in his suffering is apt—if not during crucifixion, at the very least in
his mournful prayer over Jerusalem. Compare Jesus' use of

the lament regarding the city and its future in the Gospel of Luke (13:34–35; 19:41–44; 23:27–31). "The days will come upon you," Jesus says in Luke 19:43, "when your enemies will set up ramparts around you and surround you, and hem you in on every side. They will crush you to the ground, you and your children within you, and they will not leave within you one stone upon another; because you did not recognize the time of your visitation from God."

The Jerusalem of Lamentations cries out to know why God does not intervene while Jesus links the city's future despair to its failure to recognize God's presence within it. Though God remains silent throughout the book of Lamentations, the people recognize God in the midst of sorrow, ultimately affirming, "It is good that one should wait quietly for the salvation of the Lord" (3:26).

Chapter 24
HE WAS CUT OFF
(Psalm 16:9–11)

31. Accompanied Recitative

Soprano or Tenor
He was cut off out of the land of the living:
for the transgressions of Thy people was He stricken.
(Isa. 53:8)

32. Air

Soprano or Tenor
But Thou didst not leave His soul in hell;
nor didst Thou suffer Thy Holy One to see corruption.
(Ps. 16:10)

Psalm 16:9–11

[9]Therefore my heart is glad, and my soul rejoices;
my body also rests secure.
[10]For you do not give me up to Sheol,
or let your faithful one see the Pit.

[11]You show me the path of life.
In your presence there is fullness of joy;
in your right hand are pleasures forevermore.

*O*ne of the Eastern church's best-known iconographic images is that of the risen Christ reaching down into the grave to rescue Adam and Eve. Standing on the broken gates of hell, he raises them to new life with him. The message is clear: death has been defeated once and for all through Christ who saves us.

The idea that Jesus spent the days between death and resurrection in hell, experiencing complete separation from God and/or redeeming those righteous people who had died before the Messiah's coming, is largely a matter of speculation. Paul made that assumption, saying in Ephesians 4:9, "When it says, 'He ascended,' what does it mean but that he had also descended into the lower parts of the earth?" and it soon made its way into the Apostles' Creed as well. Isaiah's description of the Suffering Servant, "He was cut off from the land of the living," seems figurative, but Handel uses the phrase to suggest Jesus' descent to Sheol before using Psalm 16:10 to narrate Christ's ascent out of the depths, back into the land of the living.

The tradition of interpreting Psalm 16, particularly verses 9–11, through a passion lens is ancient, as old as the church itself. Luke records Peter's and Paul's citing the passage in reference to Christ in Acts 2:25–28 and Acts 13:35, respectively. Peter's speech to those assembled on the day of Pentecost (Acts 2:14–36) illustrates how the writers of the New Testament used their Scripture, translated into Greek from Hebrew, to interpret what had happened in the life, death, and resurrection of Jesus. In the midrashic style of theological debate practiced in rabbinic circles, Peter cites the prophet Joel and then the psalmist to provide proof texts for his christological claims.

To Peter and Paul, Psalm 16:10 doubly proves Jesus' bodily resurrection, saying not only that God raised

Jesus up ("will not abandon [him] to Hades") but also that Jesus' body did not undergo the normal physical decomposition. It may seem to be a major overreach of the Psalm for Peter and Paul to say that God will not "let your Holy One experience corruption," referring to the disintegration of the physical body after death. It is an issue of translation. Where the psalmist writes, "You did not . . . let your faithful one see the Pit," the word *pit* appears in the Greek translation of Hebrew Scriptures as "corruption." (As the King James Bible was translated from Greek, Handel too uses "corruption," with all its bodily implications.) Peter emphasizes that implication further in Acts by replacing "faithful one" or "Holy One" with "his flesh." Peter and Paul both go on to say that because King David, the presumed psalmist, is known to have died and remained buried, Psalm 16 must be referring to one even more holy, the Lord's anointed Messiah. Unlike mere mortals, the body of God's Holy One will not stay in the earth to rot but be raised to sit at the right hand of God.

The intent of Peter's sermon and Handel's oratorio is christological; both use Psalm 16 to say something profound about the identity and nature of the Messiah, particularly his ultimate triumph over death. The intent of the psalmist's prayer is more personal. The psalmist is recalling times of need and disorientation, times of trouble that all of us experience and that may cause us even more despair as Christmas approaches. Losses of the past year and years past may haunt us more in contrast with the bright festivity of the season. In times of despair, the promise of the coming Christ child's triumph over death gives us hope, and the psalmist gives us words to express enduring faith: You, Lord, do not give me up. *You show me the path of life. In your presence, there is joy.*

Chapter 25

HE IS THE KING OF GLORY
(Psalm 24)

33. Chorus

Lift up your heads, O ye gates;
and be ye lift up, ye everlasting doors;
and the King of Glory shall come in.
Who is this King of Glory?
The Lord strong and mighty,
The Lord mighty in battle.
Lift up your heads, O ye gates;
and be ye lift up, ye everlasting doors;
and the King of Glory shall come in.
Who is this King of Glory?
The Lord of hosts, He is the King of Glory.

(Ps. 24:7–10)

Psalm 24

[1]The earth is the LORD's and all that is in it,
  the world, and those who live in it;
[2]for he has founded it on the seas,
  and established it on the rivers.

[3]Who shall ascend the hill of the LORD?
  And who shall stand in his holy place?

⁴Those who have clean hands and pure hearts,
    who do not lift up their souls to what is false,
    and do not swear deceitfully.
⁵They will receive blessing from the LORD,
    and vindication from the God of their salvation.
⁶Such is the company of those who seek him,
    who seek the face of the God of Jacob. *Selah*
⁷Lift up your heads, O gates!
    and be lifted up, O ancient doors!
    that the King of glory may come in.
⁸Who is the King of glory?
    The LORD, strong and mighty,
    the LORD, mighty in battle.
⁹Lift up your heads, O gates!
    and be lifted up, O ancient doors!
    that the King of glory may come in.
¹⁰Who is this King of glory?
    The LORD of hosts,
    he is the King of glory. *Selah*

*P*salm 24 is really two psalms, two stanzas: one is an affirmation of the Creator's creative ownership of creation; the other, a majestic anthem of praise to God's mighty rule. Both are framed by questions and answers; both suggest processions on the way to worship; both speak of divine sovereignty and human stewardship.

The psalm begins with a triumphant proclamation of God's power and immanence. It is not merely that the temple "is the LORD's," or Jerusalem "is the LORD's," or Israel "is the LORD's." This is no local deity summoning our praise; rather, this is the One who created "the earth . . . and all that is in it, the world, and those who live in it."

The claim of the psalm is vast and utterly unbounded, so we should not be constrained to interpret "the earth" and "the world" with paltry literalism.

This is no tribal God, nor God merely of the planet Earth. Physicist Carl Sagan famously provided a definition that "the cosmos is all that is or ever was or ever will be," and that sizes up the situation in which we come to worship. Contemporary physicists suggest that, given their calculations, there are not merely the four dimensions we experience (three dimensions of space and one of time) but perhaps as many as twenty-six, and certainly at least ten. What God do these dimensions serve? Physics now speaks soberly about multiple universes. Who authored these other realms, and under whose sovereignty do they spin? Psalm 24 insists they are the Lord's. If we are not dazzled and perhaps a bit dizzy from the heights proposed by the psalm and seconded by modern physics, we are not paying attention. It is all the Lord's "and the fullness thereof" (v. 1 KJV).

Stunned with such an encompassing vision, we inevitably wonder how we might worship such a God: "Who shall ascend the hill of the LORD?" Psalm 24 describes the character and disposition of worshipers: they are "pure in heart" and seek the face of God. The situation is somewhat paradoxical: those who seek to worship have been shaped by worship. "Clean hands and pure hearts" describe those who seek God.

That little, untranslatable word "*Selah*" introduces a new refrain with verse 7. If the first refrain (vv. 1–6) is an orientation toward the holiness of all creation, the second (vv. 7–10) is focused on the holy portals of the temple. The worshipers of a mighty, sovereign, majestic Lord are knocking at heaven's doors. Repentance marked the first climb up the holy hill; the second ascent is accompanied by an anthem of majesty and might.

Handel's chorus sings in our ears as we read this psalm, women's voices asking an innocent question: "Who is this King of glory?" The answer comes from the male chorus: "The LORD strong and mighty!" Worshipers are ready to enter the grand temple gates accompanied by the ark of the covenant. Worshipers are entering sacred space accompanied by their glorious, regal, warrior God. Here the sovereign God is praised for taming chaos, for military victory, but not, as before, for mercy or relationship. Only when both refrains are sung do we get a picture of divine sovereignty that tempers the controlling, victorious warrior king praised in the second stanza. Psalm 24 is a song with at least two contrapuntal themes.

God's sovereignty is ownership, transcendence, immanence, freedom, holiness, and relational power. Human faithfulness is dependence, repentance, stewardship, and worship. Created world and earthly temple are both holy, sacred space. Just how are the doors of the temple lifted? How are the gates flung wide? Imagine the masses of worshipers pushing or pulling those grand doors open. Imagine a doorkeeper pulling them open from the inside out. Imagine Holman Hunt's famous painting, in St. Paul's in London, of an ivy-covered door with no handle, the Savior knocking, waiting: "Listen! I am standing at the door, knocking" (Rev. 3:20). Imagine that entryway where "through gates of pearl streams in the countless host!"*

The gates do not open by themselves; that we know. Even the mighty warrior king does not force them open. The faithful are entreated to open the doors, to welcome

* William Walsham How, "For All the Saints," in *Glory to God: The Presbyterian Hymnal* (Louisville, KY: Westminster John Knox Press, 2013), 326.

the Creator of heaven and earth. The doors of Jerusalem's temple were real doors. In psalms and hymns and prayers and pictures these doors are imagined in many ways—from heaven's pearly gates to the doubts and fears and wounds that keep us from welcoming our free, holy, and ever-present God.

So, along with this psalm, an Advent hymn rings in our ears, affirming our grateful response to God's sovereign love:

> Fling wide the portals of your heart;
> make it a temple, set apart
> from earthly use for heaven's employ,
> adorned with prayer and love and joy.[*]

---

[*] Georg Weissel, "Lift Up Your Heads, Ye Mighty Gates," in *Glory to God: The Presbyterian Hymnal* (Louisville, KY: Westminster John Knox Press, 2013), 93.

Chapter 26

LET ALL THE ANGELS WORSHIP HIM
(Hebrews 1:1–8)

34. Recitative

Tenor
Unto which of the angels said He at any time:
"Thou art My Son, this day have I begotten Thee?"
(Heb. 1:5)

35. Chorus

Let all the angels of God worship Him.
(Heb. 1:6)

Hebrews 1:1–8

[1]Long ago God spoke to our ancestors in many and various ways by the prophets, [2]but in these last days he has spoken to us by a Son, whom he appointed heir of all things, through whom he also created the worlds. [3]He is the reflection of God's glory and the exact imprint of God's very being, and he sustains all things by his powerful word. When he had made purification for sins, he sat down at the right hand of the Majesty on high, [4]having become as much superior to angels as the name he has inherited is more excellent than theirs.

[5]For to which of the angels did God ever say,
"You are my Son;
    today I have begotten you"?
Or again,
    "I will be his Father,
    and he will be my Son"?
[6]And again, when he brings the firstborn
    into the world, he says,
"Let all God's angels worship him."
[7]Of the angels he says,
"He makes his angels winds,
and his servants flames of fire."
[8]But of the Son he says,
"Your throne, O God, is forever and ever,
and the righteous scepter is the scepter
    of your kingdom.

*H*ebrews 1 makes an astounding claim about the connection between God and flesh, body and spirit, the universal and the particular, the temporal and the eternal. It comes in verse 3: "He is the reflection of God's glory and the exact imprint of God's very being." To proclaim that in Jesus the glory of God was revealed and that Jesus (in body and spirit) was nothing less than "the exact imprint of God's very being," is to declare that flesh can no longer define existence that is not-God. Flesh is God's territory no less than spirit. The world of bodies, time, and space is God's world through and through.

The author of Hebrews makes a point of saying how, despite his flesh, Jesus is more holy, more exalted, than the other divine beings with which people would have been familiar. Angels were regarded as mediators of the revelations that gave them prophecy and the law; exalted as they are, they are but servants of God for the sake of those saved by Christ. Thus Hebrews 1:5–12 goes on to show how the revelation in Christ fulfills Scripture in being superior to the angels and their ministry.

Interestingly, those whom Jesus is "superior to" or "more excellent than" receive greater air time than Jesus does in this sermon's opening move. If the angels are of such relatively inferior importance to the Son, why does the author of Hebrews go on so long about them? Perhaps because, one way or another, angels have a way of stealing the show (even if that is not really their fault).

It is well and good to describe Jesus in sweeping cosmic terms (as the writer of the Fourth Gospel also does), but the cosmos is hard to observe with the naked eye. So it is perhaps not surprising that celestial creatures more strikingly depicted can be more attention grabbing—particularly since God's anointed one actually looks pretty ordinary under the best of human circumstances and ends up looking not at all pretty. As the words of Isaiah suggest (53:2):

> He had no form or majesty that we should look at him,
>   nothing in his appearance that we should desire him.

Angel gazing is always alive and well—a thriving business, both commercially and spiritually. Take an image count from Christmas cards, wrapping paper, holiday displays, and seasonal carols. Angels almost always come out on top. (The majority of Holy Family images are bedecked with angelic halos!) Take a survey of how much Christmas sermon language (beginning with Scripture) relies on angels (or stars) in proportion (if not preference) to the factors and features of the mundane life the Son comes to inhabit.

Angels can be energizing (in an entertaining sort of way), but they can seem to be sources of the life for which they are only ministers. The true source, God in Christ, is much messier but ultimately much more amazing. Christology at its highest reveals the mystery of a God who bridges height and depth, temporality and eternity, flesh and spirit, divinity and humanity. It is the truth of incarnation that keeps us awake and alert to the possibility of the glory of God in the flesh of humanity—even our own.

For all our talk about spirit and spirituality, it is bodily life that preoccupies much of our attention. The prayers offered in worship on any given Sunday reveal our yearning to know God's grace and presence in relation to our physical lives—bodily health, safety, and security. Our needs are more than just spiritual, so God came to earth in more than just spiritual form. This is a principal theme to be developed in later passages in the Letter to the Hebrews: "Since, therefore, the children share flesh and blood, he himself likewise shared the same things" (Heb. 2:14). "Therefore he had to become like his brothers and sisters in every respect, so that he might be a merciful and faithful high priest" (Heb. 2:17). "For we do not have a high priest who is unable to sympathize with our weaknesses" (Heb. 4:15).

Angels may shine with God's glory, but our hope and healing come through a God unafraid to trod with us in the muck and mire of earth.

Chapter 27
EVEN FROM THINE ENEMIES
(Psalm 68:1–12, 17–20)

36. Air

Alto or Soprano
Thou art gone up on high;
Thou hast led captivity captive,
and received gifts for men;
yea, even from Thine enemies,
that the Lord God might dwell among them.

(Ps. 68:18)

37. Chorus

The Lord gave the word:
great was the company of the preachers.

(Ps. 68:11)

Psalm 68:1–12, 17–20

¹Let God rise up, let his enemies be scattered;
  let those who hate him flee before him.
²As smoke is driven away, so drive them away;
  as wax melts before the fire,
  let the wicked perish before God.

³But let the righteous be joyful;
  let them exult before God;
  let them be jubilant with joy.

⁴Sing to God, sing praises to his name;
  lift up a song to him who rides upon the clouds—
his name is the LORD—
  be exultant before him.

⁵Father of orphans and protector of widows
  is God in his holy habitation.
⁶God gives the desolate a home to live in;
  he leads out the prisoners to prosperity,
  but the rebellious live in a parched land.

⁷O God, when you went out before your people,
  when you marched through the wilderness, *Selah*
⁸the earth quaked, the heavens poured down rain
  at the presence of God, the God of Sinai,
  at the presence of God, the God of Israel.
⁹Rain in abundance, O God, you showered abroad;
  you restored your heritage when it languished;
¹⁰your flock found a dwelling in it;
  in your goodness, O God, you provided for the
    needy.

¹¹The Lord gives the command;
  great is the company of those who bore the tidings:
  ¹² "The kings of the armies, they flee, they flee!"
The women at home divide the spoil, . . .

. . . .

¹⁷With mighty chariotry, twice ten thousand,
  thousands upon thousands,
  the Lord came from Sinai into the holy place.

¹⁸You ascended the high mount,
  leading captives in your train
  and receiving gifts from people,
even from those who rebel against the LORD God's
  abiding there.
¹⁹Blessed be the Lord,
  who daily bears us up;
  God is our salvation. *Selah*
²⁰Our God is a God of salvation,
  and to GOD, the LORD, belongs escape from death.

Psalm 68 depicts God as a triumphant military leader punishing the wicked who deservingly lost the battle. The psalmist draws distinction as if etched in neon between the righteous and those who hate God. The enemies of God flee and melt and perish while the righteous are "jubilant with joy." The psalmist speaks of a clear division between the righteous and the unrighteous. We know from our experience that in flesh and blood these lines are never drawn so neatly. Such unambiguous divisions are reserved for old-time western movies in which the bad guys wear black hats and the heroes wear white hats. In the drama of our living we never leave a trail of faithfulness with such clarity. The human heart is the garden for both weed and wheat.

Read in individual verses, as in Handel's use of this psalm, these triumphant depictions of God can be edifying. Generally, however, a God known for protecting and parenting some and scattering and melting others is not a welcome image for most of us, especially in light of Christ, who said to love our enemies, not shatter their heads, as Psalm 68:21 goes on to say.

However, for those who know the world to have crushed them, for those who live on the bottom, this language of certainty is the only prayer that rings authentic. Sometimes the only prayer we can pray from the pit is that our enemies would perish. From the bottom, we pray for God to make things right, to set things straight, to destroy death and all the tools of death. This song belongs to the lowly. It may not offer a literal description of God's way in this world, but it does provide a picture of the only prayers we sometimes know from the bottom.

More and more, our understanding of God is defined by what some would call our "experience" of God. We sing of God as protector and home because we have experienced God as the same, but this is not the case for the psalmist. The confession of God's protection is rooted not in the soil of the psalmist's own experience but rather in the shared memory of the faith community. These holy memories empower the psalmist to engage in a work of holy imagination that is born not of the present experience of the faithful but from the testimony of previous faith communities. The psalmist remembers the difficult journey Israel has had with God—promise and slavery, the wilderness wandering and the gift of the law at Sinai, the land and the invasions they've endured. Reciting this journey, this story of God's faithfulness, empowers the psalmist to praise.

The psalm parallels the confession Christian people make. We gather to remember the work of God not simply in our own experience but in the journey of the church. Because God raised Jesus Christ from the dead, we have a narrative of hope to proclaim, even if we find ourselves among the weak and lowly. We remember what God has done and therefore profess with joy what God will do.

Faith will lack power to carry us through the valley of the shadow if it is not claimed personally. Faith is rooted in the experience of the believing one, but God cannot be limited to my experience alone because God is bigger than my experience of God. Particularly when God's people lift prayers and praise from the pit, particularly when we cry out to God burdened by the cross we are called to carry, we must lean into the full story of God's faithfulness. It can place into our own mouths the language of praise.

"Let God rise up. Ascribe power to God, the rider in the heavens. Blessed be God." This is the language of praise, uttered by those who know the powers that erode and seek to destroy life and yet have come to know God as one who comes as an innocent baby and calls the walking dead to breathe again in new life.

Chapter 28
HOW BEAUTIFUL
(Romans 10:8–15)

38. Air

Soprano or Alto
How beautiful are the feet of them
that preach the gospel of peace,
and bring glad tidings of good things.
(Isa. 52:7; Rom. 10:15)

Romans 10:8–15

[8]What does it say?
"The word is near you,
    on your lips and in your heart"
(that is, the word of faith that we proclaim); [9]because
if you confess with your lips that Jesus is Lord and
believe in your heart that God raised him from the
dead, you will be saved. [10]For one believes with the
heart and so is justified, and one confesses with the
mouth and so is saved. [11]The scripture says, "No
one who believes in him will be put to shame." [12]For
there is no distinction between Jew and Greek; the
same Lord is Lord of all and is generous to all who
call on him. [13]For, "Everyone who calls on the name
of the Lord shall be saved."

[14]But how are they to call on one in whom they have not believed? And how are they to believe in one of whom they have never heard? And how are they to hear without someone to proclaim him? [15]And how are they to proclaim him unless they are sent? As it is written, "How beautiful are the feet of those who bring good news!"

*"H*ow beautiful are the feet of those who bring good news." With this citation of Isaiah 52:7, Paul discloses to the Romans his goal for Jesus' followers not just to believe the gospel but to proclaim it. Evangelism has come to be a kind of dirty word in some churches, something uncomfortable at best and embarrassing at worst. It is somehow not seemly to go around airing one's personal faith to others, especially those who might not share that faith. Evangelism is one of those ideas that has somehow lost its way, at least in some religious circles; it has come to be associated with itinerant preachers, tent revivals, and fundamentalists—expressions of faith and ministry that seem out of place in our modern world, even offensive to some.

This is odd because, in its broadest sense, evangelism is the work of those who are messengers of good news. The word itself has the same roots as *angel*. No matter what the times are like, we could all use a little good news; we could all benefit from more angels around us. Why then should it be so difficult for some churches to engage in evangelism and to support those who would talk about their own faith?

Evangelism is something that must always happen in context; there is no one-size-fits-all approach. Some consider mission to be the most acceptable form of evangelism while others are more comfortable going out and talking about faith, even in public, secular places. Even though they are different, both forms of evangelism—social justice and verbal witnessing—are equally valid, and there are ample opportunities for both at Christmastime. The needs of so many are heightened this time of year, as budgets are strained and temperatures plummet, and conversations about the holiday commemorating Jesus' birth provide opportunities to share what the incarnation means to us.

The tension around evangelism is not from the methods employed but rather from the motives. Those who feel that their actions can "save" others, whether those actions be good works or persuasive words, have missed the mark. Paul offers a gentle correction to those who would bring Christ to others. He reminds us that Christ is already present. It is not up to us to save the world. God has already done that. We cannot save others by our actions alone. We cannot even save ourselves (vv. 5–7).

Some people will be comforted by this message. They will see it as permission to sit back and let God do the work of salvation. It will feel like an easy way out. Others will find the whole discussion of salvation to be old-fashioned and not especially relevant for the complex issues facing the church and the world in the twenty-first century. For many Christians, though, a thoughtful consideration of Paul's teaching will raise big questions: If God in Christ has already done it all, then what are we supposed to do? What is our purpose in the world? What does it mean to "confess with our lips" and "believe in our hearts"?

It is important to understand that neither private piety nor street-corner sermons will do. What the apostle is urging is a life of interior and exterior authenticity, a life based on faith. We may not be able to change anything, but faith can change everything. Where faith is concerned, being and doing are not polarities; instead, they are opposite sides of the same coin. Just as no one has a monopoly on the gracious abundance of the Lord's love, so those who know that love in their very being are to ensure that others do too.

Faith is an embodied reality. In this brief passage alone, Paul speaks of lips (vv. 8–9), mouth (v. 10), heart (v. 8–10), and feet (v. 15). The way for believers to explain God to those who have not heard is not through theological brilliance, scriptural proofs, or doctrine and dogma. Instead, it is living out the word that is within (v. 8) and doing so in a way that makes sense in context. Even God, according to John Calvin, accommodates God's unknowable majesty to our finitude: "God is wont in a measure to 'lisp' in speaking to us."*

We are to do the same, framing our message so it can be understood—human to human, somebody to another body. Depending on the context, this could mean witnessing to one's own faith by speaking about it or by engaging in actions that proclaim that faith in concrete ways. In any case, the instruction of Scripture is clear: those who believe are to be messengers of the good news of faith.

* John Calvin, *Institutes of the Christian Religion*, 1.13.1; ed. John T. McNeill, trans. Ford Lewis Battles, Library of Christian Classics (Philadelphia: Westminster Press, 1960).

Chapter 29
INTO ALL LANDS
(Psalm 19)

39. Chorus

Their sound is gone out into all lands,
and their words unto the ends of the world.
(Rom. 10:18; Ps. 19:4)

Psalm 19

[1]The heavens are telling the glory of God;
    and the firmament proclaims his handiwork.
[2]Day to day pours forth speech,
    and night to night declares knowledge.
[3]There is no speech, nor are there words;
    their voice is not heard;
[4]yet their voice goes out through all the earth,
    and their words to the end of the world.

In the heavens he has set a tent for the sun,
[5]which comes out like a bridegroom from his
    wedding canopy,
    and like a strong man runs its course with joy.
[6]Its rising is from the end of the heavens,
    and its circuit to the end of them;
    and nothing is hid from its heat.

⁷The law of the LORD is perfect,
   reviving the soul;
the decrees of the LORD are sure,
   making wise the simple;
⁸the precepts of the LORD are right,
   rejoicing the heart;
the commandment of the LORD is clear,
   enlightening the eyes;
⁹the fear of the LORD is pure,
   enduring forever;
the ordinances of the LORD are true
   and righteous altogether.
¹⁰More to be desired are they than gold,
   even much fine gold;
sweeter also than honey,
   and drippings of the honeycomb.

¹¹Moreover by them is your servant warned;
   in keeping them there is great reward.
¹²But who can detect their errors?
   Clear me from hidden faults.
¹³Keep back your servant also from the insolent;
   do not let them have dominion over me.
Then I shall be blameless,
   and innocent of great transgression.

¹⁴Let the words of my mouth and the meditation
   of my heart
   be acceptable to you,
O LORD, my rock and my redeemer.

*P*salm 19 takes us through the three distinct moments that, in the psalmist's view, are central to the worshipful life. In the first moment, we are invited to recall the witness given to God's splendor by the textures and glory of creation (vv. 1–6). The second moment reminds us of the significance and wonder of God's law (vv. 7–10). Finally, the psalmist calls us to the humble recognition of human frailty and limitation in the face of these majestic glories and of the need for God's grace (vv. 11–14).

Psalm 19 is a particularly elegant example of how God leads humanity to perfection through forms of speech. That is to say, the Psalms exemplify words and speech (and, of course, music) as a medium through which God "speaks" into creation, and they illustrate how creation through its very character "speaks" as a witness to God. This dimension of Psalm 19 led Calvin to refer to the heavens as "preachers" of the glory of God. Understood in this way, the psalm is an important reminder of two facets of the relationship between revelation and Scripture. In the first place, the psalm helpfully recalls the fact that God's voice has not been locked up as prisoner in the print of Scripture. In times of rampant bibliolatry (idolization of the Bible), it is a reminder that God is still speaking through the majesty of creation—both "nature" and humanity—with words of blessing and judgment.

Beyond drawing us to appreciate the power of creation to bear witness to God, this psalm also entreats us to see the law of God as a thing of beauty and sweetness. While the psalmist had Torah in mind, Christian interpreters might think of the broad stream of Christian wisdom encompassed in the tradition and practices of our faith communities. We may bristle at this idea, and indeed, legalists of every age have sought to make the law something onerous—as when it is reduced to a selective reading of Scripture and then used as a cudgel in culture wars. Here the psalmist invites us to another understanding, namely, of the law of God as the way-making and sense-making word of guidance. This word of God, while borne witness to by the majesty of the heavens and all of creation, is never reducible to any "thing" in creation. So the church, its traditions, and its Scripture must always be understood as parts of God's address to us but never confused with that address in its totality. For even while God is revealed to us in Christ's advent on earth, even then God still speaks though the majesty of creation, the mysteries of love, and, as Handel implies by using this Psalm adjacent to Romans 10:15, the faithful witness of disciples down through the ages.

The psalmist goes on to observe how human frailty and weakness impede our knowledge of God and the wisdom to contemplate how we might please God. In identifying these frailties, the psalmist takes the important step of naming the faults that are secret or invisible to us (v. 12)—the sins that emerge from presumption—as sins of the first order, from which God's protection is needed. In our contemporary context, these sins might be thought of as distorted worldviews or misguided cultural practices and beliefs (i.e., racism, classism, and sexism). On the psalmist's account these frailties make us vulnerable to the dominion of evil-doers.

Beyond the invisible sins of custom and common sense, the psalmist also reflects on the sins of willfulness and self-centeredness. Several translators read the psalmist as naming this as the path to the "great transgression," which we might read as living our lives under the dominion of any but God. It is here, with the identification of our willfulness in the face of this display, that the psalmist invites us to see how our failure to see and hear God in creation ultimately leads to our downfall.

At Christmas, it is all the more important to remember that when the Word took on flesh, it was precisely the flesh of creation that was taken on. So, far from relativizing or discounting creation, we have all the more reason to experience the Divine flowing through it.

Chapter 30

WHY DO THE NATIONS RAGE?
(Psalm 2:1–3, 7–8)

40. Air

Bass

Why do the nations so furiously rage together,
and why do the people imagine a vain thing?
The kings of the earth rise up,
and the rulers take counsel together
against the Lord, and against His Anointed.

(Ps. 2:1–2)

41. Chorus

Let us break their bonds asunder,
and cast away their yokes from us.

(Ps. 2:3)

Psalm 2:1–3, 7–8

¹Why do the nations conspire,
    and the peoples plot in vain?
²The kings of the earth set themselves,
    and the rulers take counsel together,
    against the LORD and his anointed, saying,
³"Let us burst their bonds asunder,
    and cast their cords from us."

· · · · · · · · · ·

> ⁷I will tell of the decree of the LORD:
> He said to me, "You are my son;
>   today I have begotten you.
> ⁸Ask of me, and I will make the nations your heritage,
>   and the ends of the earth your possession."

Psalm 2 is widely understood to be a royal psalm that most likely was composed for a royal coronation in Jerusalem. It refers to earthly kings and includes words of consecration. The psalm opens with a rhetorical question, taunting the nations for their foolish and impotent conspiracies against the power and authority of the Israelite God and his anointed. As a coronation psalm, the text affirms the consolidation of the new king's power in the face of rebellious vassals. The "anointed one" (*mashiach*, or messiah) is a royal title in ancient Israel; in later Jewish and Christian tradition, it signifies an eschatological savior. Since the days of the early church, Christians have understood the reference to messiah as foretelling Jesus Christ as the Messiah who is divinely enthroned after his resurrection.

With the psalm's original, ancient context in mind, Psalm 2 invites us to consider rulers and their use of power in our contemporary world. Verses 1–3 attest to the tendency of those in positions of authority to abuse their power. Throughout history and now, we see examples of such abuse. Sometimes they are atrocities, such as genocide committed under the regime of a dictator. Other times, as we see more often in the United States, the abuses are more subtle—the politician who takes a lavish trip on the taxpayers' dime, for example.

Even if we are not monarchs or elected officials, Psalm 2 includes warnings for us as well. All of us have power of some sort, and inherent in us is that same human tendency to crave power. The famous Stanford prison experiment illustrates this. In 1971, a Stanford psychologist and his team of researchers wanted to learn more about the psychological effects of being a prison guard or a prisoner. They had students live in a mock prison. After just a few days, some of the "guards" became sadistic, and many of the "prisoners" began to show signs of depression and extreme stress after being subjected to brutal treatment. The results were so disconcerting that the psychologist was concerned about the well-being of those involved and consequently terminated the study early. Since then, the experiment has been an archetype for how quickly our desire for power can corrupt the humanity for which we were made.

How are we called to use and understand our power? Leading or holding power of any kind must be understood as serving God. Too often, people profess a humble faith and attend church on Sunday while failing to live out that faith in their use of power Monday through Friday. Our faith must determine how we use our power; the two are inseparable. In fact, is this not the case for all aspects of our lives? The journey of discipleship asks that we devote all that we do to serving God.

The psalm's most remarkable line quotes a divine oracle to the king: "I will tell of the decree of the LORD: He said to me, 'You are my son; today I have begotten you'" (v. 7). The text employs the common Hebrew verb for giving birth or fathering children. Although ancient Near Eastern ideas of divine kingship sometimes depict a physical relationship between the gods and the king, ancient Israelite royal ideology's use of the metaphor is better described as adoption. It is likely that this line was part of an ancient cultic rite in which the Davidic king was formally adopted by God to act as "son" or representative. The New Testament quotes Psalm 2:7 as testimony to Jesus as the Son of God, and God identifies Jesus as "my Son" at his baptism and transfiguration.

Jesus, humble in spite of his anointed status, miraculous powers, and subsequent fame, serves as a model for how we should use our own power. Through his life and in his death, Jesus channels his power not for his own glory but in service and obedience to God. Whatever earthly power we may have ultimately is nothing compared to the power of God. Our human sense of being in control is an illusion; all our plots are "in vain." This is not a loss. Rather, the knowledge that it is God—not we—who is in control comes as a huge relief. This relinquishing of power is the joy of the life of faith. While we are called to serve with fear, trembling, and awe at the mighty power of God, we do so with the peace that comes with knowing everything rests in the hands of our loving, liberating, and life-giving God. As the psalm concludes, "Happy are all who take refuge in him" (v. 12).

Chapter 31
THE LORD SHALL BREAK THEM
(Psalm 2:4-6, 9-12)

42. Recitative

Tenor
He that dwelleth in Heav'n
shall laugh them to scorn;
The Lord shall have them in derision.

(Ps. 2:4)

43. Air

Tenor
Thou shalt break them with a rod of iron;
thou shalt dash them in pieces like a potter's vessel.

(Ps. 2:9)

Psalm 2:4-6, 9-12

[4]He who sits in the heavens laughs;
    the LORD has them in derision.
[5]Then he will speak to them in his wrath,
    and terrify them in his fury, saying,
[6]"I have set my king on Zion, my holy hill."

. . . .

[9]"You shall break them with a rod of iron,
    and dash them in pieces like a potter's vessel."

> [10]Now therefore, O kings, be wise;
>   be warned, O rulers of the earth.
> [11]Serve the LORD with fear,
>   with trembling [12]kiss his feet,
> or he will be angry, and you will perish in the way;
>   for his wrath is quickly kindled.
>
> Happy are all who take refuge in him.

*T*his psalm, like several others, celebrates the anointing of God's chosen king. It may be just another in a series of kings, or it may be the promised messiah. Psalm 2 envisions this chosen king as a powerful military leader, ready to conquer the nations of the earth with the aid of God's wrathful fury (vv. 5–6, 8–9). The Lord mocks the people in their vain attempts at power and control, knowing that with little effort, the one the Lord has chosen will snap them like twigs, shatter them like glass.

This is one image of the expected messiah; indeed, it is the dominant image recorded in Hebrew Scripture. With a few notable exceptions, this is also the vision of leadership most commonly embraced by the Israelite kings and proclaimed by the prophets. This is the messiah for whom they longed.

Jesus would not conform to this expectation, however. He would not become the type of messiah that Israel anticipated. In a sense, Psalm 2 paints a picture of the path not chosen. Again and again, Jesus rejects the mantle of a powerful, militaristic messiah. We see this most notably in the familiar Gospel story of the temptation of Jesus, a temptation that this psalm almost foreshadows. Consider verses 8–9 of the psalm, in which God promises to grant the king possession over the ends of the earth and power over the nations. Place those verses alongside the dramatic scene from Luke's Gospel where the devil shows Jesus the kingdoms of the world and suggests that they could all be his (Luke 4:5–7). You can almost see the devil's sinister smile as he makes his appeal. Ironically, the psalm mirrors that image; only it is God's laughter that we hear, mocking the feeble rulers of the nations (v. 4).

The Gospels tell us that Jesus rebukes the devil. Jesus has come to reveal a different kingdom, one defined not by power and might but by humility and servanthood. Jesus repeatedly signals that his mission is not about earthly glory. When Jesus appears transfigured with Moses and Elijah, Peter wants to enshrine the three on that blessed mountaintop, to stay and worship. But instead of basking in radiance, Jesus rebukes Peter and leads the disciples back down the mountain, for he knows that his throne is not of this world and that his true glory will be revealed on the cross.

Jesus does indeed become a king on a holy hill (Ps. 2:6), but it is the hill of Golgotha, not Zion. That day, he is clothed in shame, not in splendor. That day, we hear not God laughing in derision (v. 4) but rather the crowds mocking Jesus. That day, all messianic expectations are overturned as the anointed one is crucified.

This contrast—between the expected messiah foreshadowed by Psalm 2 and the unexpected Messiah that Jesus becomes—is fruitful material for reflection. This reversal of human expectations is a key element of the scriptural narrative, but it remains counterintuitive. It was hard for people of Jesus' day to understand, and it is hard for us today. We spend so much time and energy striving for success, for esteem, for power and control; that is how we define our earthly kingdoms. In contrast, Jesus' life

and mission are defined by a relinquishing of power and
a sacrificial journey toward death. We confess and somehow believe that God acted in him to overcome death with
life. In his journey toward the cross, Jesus, the unexpected
Messiah, reveals a kingdom more eternal and more powerful than any the world has known.

Among twentieth-century Christian writers, Menno-
nite theologian John Howard Yoder stands out in his analy-
sis of this unexpected kingdom and its lessons for us. In
The Politics of Jesus Yoder demonstrates how Jesus defies
the traditional expectations of a messiah and forges a different kind of kingdom, the kingdom of God.* This kingdom
does not depend on military might or economic prowess
but rather is made known through concern for the poor,
justice for the oppressed, and love for friends and enemies
alike. In this kingdom, Jesus introduces a new social ethic,
rooted not in a quest for power and control but in a commitment to servanthood and sacrifice. It is truly an upside-
down kingdom where the last shall be first and where
suffering and death lie unavoidably on the path toward joy
and lasting life.

* John Howard Yoder, *The Politics of Jesus*, 2nd ed. (Grand Rapids: Eerdmans, 1994),
32.

Chapter 32

HALLELUJAH
(Revelation 19:6–16)

44. Chorus

Hallelujah:
for the Lord God Omnipotent reigneth.
(Rev. 19:6)

The kingdom of this world
is become the kingdom of our Lord,
and of His Christ;
and He shall reign for ever and ever.
(Rev. 11:15)

King of Kings, and Lord of Lords.
(Rev. 19:16)

Revelation 19:6–16

[6]Then I heard what seemed to be the voice of a great
multitude, like the sound of many waters and like the
sound of mighty thunderpeals, crying out,
"Hallelujah!
For the Lord our God
    the Almighty reigns.
[7] Let us rejoice and exult
    and give him the glory,

for the marriage of the Lamb has come,
　　and his bride has made herself ready;
⁸to her it has been granted to be clothed
　　with fine linen, bright and pure"—
for the fine linen is the righteous deeds of the saints.

⁹And the angel said to me, "Write this: Blessed are those who are invited to the marriage supper of the Lamb." And he said to me, "These are true words of God." ¹⁰Then I fell down at his feet to worship him, but he said to me, "You must not do that! I am a fellow servant with you and your comrades who hold the testimony of Jesus. Worship God! For the testimony of Jesus is the spirit of prophecy."

¹¹Then I saw heaven opened, and there was a white horse! Its rider is called Faithful and True, and in righteousness he judges and makes war. ¹²His eyes are like a flame of fire, and on his head are many diadems; and he has a name inscribed that no one knows but himself. ¹³He is clothed in a robe dipped in blood, and his name is called The Word of God. ¹⁴And the armies of heaven, wearing fine linen, white and pure, were following him on white horses. ¹⁵From his mouth comes a sharp sword with which to strike down the nations, and he will rule them with a rod of iron; he will tread the wine press of the fury of the wrath of God the Almighty. ¹⁶On his robe and on his thigh he has a name inscribed, "King of kings and Lord of lords."

*I*n her memoir *Evolving in Monkey Town*, author Rachel Held Evans writes, "Sometimes I think that John the

Revelator might have been a crazy old man whose creative writing assignment for the Patmos Learning Annex accidentally made it into the Bible."* Evans's wit gives voice to what many of us have probably thought about the book of Revelation. John of Patmos describes so many outrageous beasts and colorful tableaus that his apocalyptic letter could seem to be more the product of an overactive imagination than inspired revelation.

The book of Revelation is neither the mad fantasy of an obsessive paranoiac nor a divinely dictated plan for the future. Revelation is, at its heart, a book of consolation, a vision of comfort for a people persecuted and in distress. John of Patmos, exiled during a time of severe persecution, writes a letter of comfort to seven churches undergoing persecution, urging their members to remain steadfast and assuring them that despite all appearance to the contrary, the Roman Empire's power is not absolute; it is God who reigns supreme.

God's supremacy is Handel's emphasis as well, and he makes use of two angelic orations in his iconic "Hallelujah Chorus." Revelation 11:15, which provides the middle portion of the chorus ("The kingdom of this world . . .") is the angels' pronouncement at the seventh trumpet, just before the heavenly temple is opened and the ark of the covenant revealed. Revelation 19, from which the first and last lines of the chorus are drawn, begins the climax of John's apocalypse. Before the Word of God appears triumphant on a white horse, the multitude repeatedly shouts, "Hallelujah," which means "Praise the Lord." With closed eyes, one easily imagines the concert hall as the gates of heaven,

* Evans, Rachel Held. *Evolving in Monkey Town: How a Girl Who Knew All the Answers Learned to Ask the Questions.* (Grand Rapids: Zondervan Publishing House, 2010). 121.

the audience as overwhelmed as John with the majesty of the heavenly host's song of praise.

This imagining of God's ultimate victory would have been comforting to the imperiled early Christians. It is often hard for Western Christians to imagine what persecution might be like—a life lived in fear and trembling, always on the run, always faithful, never sure. It is the kind of life that the emperor Diocletian inflicted on the early Christians who wrote and preserved this book. They were the first saints of the church, brothers and sisters in the faith, risking all that they had for the sake of a name— the name of Christ, which they knew was above all other names, including the name of the emperor himself. For Diocletian, what was at stake was a matter of state control, including control of the religious imagination. For Christians, control of their inmost identity was at stake. In putting on Christ in baptism, they had been made citizens of a heavenly city, a city not made by human hands, and could do no other than act in the name of the Christ for whom they themselves were named, the Alpha and the Omega, the beginning and the end.

They were Jews become Christians in a Roman world, members of a heretical wing of a minority faith barely tolerated by a brutal empire. How these people suffered, how they recanted, how they died, how they escaped such persecution—of these matters very little is known to us. But through John's letter, we do know how they imagined their freedom, should it ever come. And even after two millennia, in this startling vision of God's triumph, contemporary Christians can catch a glimpse of their own fears and their own hopes. What these people saw was extraordinary. No matter what things looked like at the moment, a greater reality held sway:

The emperor rules most of the known world?
The Lord, the Omnipotent God, reigns over all.

The kingdom of the world oppresses and
  persecutes us?
*The kingdom of the world will soon be the kingdom of
  our Lord, and of his anointed one.*

These trials seem interminable?
The Lord's reign will last for ever and ever.

Kings and lords hold all the power?
He is King of kings and Lord of Lords.

Hail Caesar?
Praise the Lord.

PART 3

CHRIST'S ETERNAL REIGN

Chapter 33
MY REDEEMER LIVETH
(Job 19:23–27)

45. Air (Part 1)

Soprano
I know that my Redeemer liveth,
and that He shall stand
at the latter day upon the earth.
And though worms destroy this body,
yet in my flesh shall I see God.

(Job 19:25–26)

Job 19:23-27

[23]"O that my words were written down!
   O that they were inscribed in a book!
[24]O that with an iron pen and with lead
   they were engraved on a rock forever!
[25]For I know that my Redeemer lives,
   and that at the last he will stand upon the earth;
[26]and after my skin has been thus destroyed,
   then in my flesh I shall see God,
[27]whom I shall see on my side,
   and my eyes shall behold, and not another.
   My heart faints within me!"

*A*n absolutely essential road sign to observe while driving through the rugged terrain of the book of Job is "Beware of lovely affirmations of faith." With Handel's soprano air ringing in our ears, this road sign flashes neon yellow when we are approaching Job 19:25. If we fail to pay attention to the road sign, we will be inspired by Handel but will detour around the rich theological claims and challenges of this perplexing text from Job. Whether or not the persecuted first generations of Christians sought inspiration from Job, Handel uses Job's affirmation of faith as a response to the soul-lifting shouts of "Hallelujah," as the individual claims belief in God's ultimate triumph in spite of whatever pain he or she may endure in this life.

Reading (or singing) these verses out of context can distort our understanding of the Job story. Admittedly, it is hard to stay on the Joban road with all its theological pot- holes and faded road markings. The detours are much more alluring, for on the Joban road there is so much carnage, so many gruesome sights, so much human agony. They are the last thing anyone wants to dwell on, especially at Christmas, but losing sight of the text's hazardous context can cheapen our affirmations of faith and perpetuate the lies that the faithful do not suffer and the suffering lack faith.

Suffering calls into question all notions of the charac- ter of God: Does suffering exist because God does not care or is not aware of it or because God is not all powerful and cannot prevent it? Does God care but choose not to prevent it because it is somehow necessary or good? Throughout the book of Job, Job seems certain that God is aware of his suffering, but Job never resolves the perennial question of why he suffers.

In verses 23–24 Job expresses his longing for a per- manent record of his suffering. He wants the story written down, inscribed, engraved. It is important to this sufferer that knowledge of God's role in his suffering be available for all time, for all people. Though the question of why suffering happens seems unanswerable for Job (and for us), a helpful understanding for those who suffer loudly as well as for those who suffer silently centers around God's presence. Job's permanent record is not essential. God hears the pain of those who struggle internally, those who seem unable to articulate their pain, with the same acuity as God hears those who announce and record their pain. God is equally present to the noisy and the numb.

Early in chapter 19, Job pleads for pity from his friends but not from God. Job's need for a redeemer who intercedes for him indicates that Job is unable or unwilling to plead for pity from God on his own behalf. The necessity of a redeemer or intercessor to act on behalf of the sufferer indicates Job's vulnerability. He is so overwhelmed by pain that he is unable to voice his need to God. Suffering by definition brings vulnerability. Redemption by definition requires sacrifice, something given by the redeemer on behalf of the redeemed. Job, however, offers no clue as to the nature of his redeemer or the redeemer's sacrifice on his behalf, only that his redeemer or vindicator lives and at the last will stand on the earth. Victorious and alive in the end, Job's redeemer, who delivers from suffering, here resembles Christ, who delivers from sin.

Job's suffering is not, however, a result of Job's sin. His redeemer, therefore, does not seek forgiveness or deliverance for Job's sin, the focus of Christ's redemption, but instead seeks deliverance for Job from his suffering. The focus of this understanding of redemption is different but meaningful for Christians. This different understanding of redemption calls us not only to lift up Christ as a forgiver of sins but also to offer ourselves to work toward the alleviation of suffering in our world. Though it is Christ's role as redeemer to forgive sin, when we act to relieve suffering, we act as redeemers on God's behalf.

Chapter 34

FOR NOW CHRIST IS RISEN
(1 Corinthians 15:12-20)

45. Air (Part 2)

Soprano
For now is Christ risen from the dead,
the first fruits of them that sleep.
                    (1 Cor. 15:20)

1 Corinthians 15:12-20

¹²Now if Christ is proclaimed as raised from the dead,
how can some of you say there is no resurrection of
the dead? ¹³If there is no resurrection of the dead,
then Christ has not been raised; ¹⁴and if Christ has
not been raised, then our proclamation has been in
vain and your faith has been in vain. ¹⁵We are even
found to be misrepresenting God, because we testified of God that he raised Christ—whom he did not
raise if it is true that the dead are not raised. ¹⁶For
if the dead are not raised, then Christ has not been
raised. ¹⁷If Christ has not been raised, your faith is
futile and you are still in your sins. ¹⁸Then those also
who have died in Christ have perished. ¹⁹If for this
life only we have hoped in Christ, we are of all people
most to be pitied.

²⁰

²⁰But in fact Christ has been raised from the dead, the first fruits of those who have died.

*I*n his correspondence with the Corinthians, Paul has learned that some within the church doubt the truth of the resurrection. Others are worried about what has happened to those who have died before the return of Christ. For Paul, everything stands or falls on the resurrection. Their disbelief in the resurrection of the dead runs directly counter to the heart of his proclamation. Paul has inextricably linked the resurrection of Jesus Christ with the general resurrection of the dead. If there is no resurrection of the dead, and if Christ has not been raised from the dead, then the faith of the church is empty and without meaning.

In this scientific age, people know all about the processes of nature. On television and computer screens everyone can watch the cycle of natural life from birth to death and from death to decay. Modern medicine can resuscitate a body in certain circumstances, but no one has ever seen anyone raised from the dead who does not die again. People know the philosophical arguments against life after death; in this context, the testimony of the church can seem like a quaint myth left over from a former age. In addition, bodily existence is a problem for many people. Chronic pain, life-threatening cancers, loss of pregnancies, and the death of loved ones make physical life precarious at best and torture at worst. Beyond the personal experience of death, instant communications have made almost everyone keenly aware of the vast scale of human tragedies in our local communities and in the world. Can God truly value physical existence when so many people die of abuse, random violence, genocide, and famine?

Like for some of the Corinthians, belief in an escape from this bodily existence to some higher disembodied afterlife sounds like a good idea. How much more pleasant it is to contemplate the immortality of the soul than this messy business of bodily resurrection. But, as God demonstrated through the incarnation, God is not above the messy business of physical life.

There is every reason in the world to question, doubt, and disbelieve the resurrection, except one: "But in fact Christ has been raised from the dead, the first fruits of those who have died." Since the resurrection of the body stands at the core of the Christian proclamation, the implications of this belief touch every area of congregational life and ministry.

First of all, the belief in the resurrection is an affirmation of the whole life of Jesus. Without the resurrection, the Christian faith can be reduced to little more than a moral code to guide well-meaning people about how to live their lives. How could anyone know that what Jesus said and what Jesus did are worth following? It is the resurrection that makes sense of the life and teachings of Jesus. Only in the light of the resurrection can believers understand the paradox of saving one's life by losing one's life. Only in the light of the resurrection does it make sense for followers of Jesus to stand with the poor, the outcasts, and the oppressed. The doctrine of the resurrection invites people to join Christ in providing care and seeking justice for the most vulnerable people in our society and trusting that God will bless these efforts, even when the results cannot be seen. The resurrection gives the faithful the freedom to live their lives in the shadow of the cross, as Jesus did. The hope of the church is not confined to this world.

The belief in the resurrection of the body is an affirmation of the significance of human life as a part of the created world. Human existence is bound up in the life of the material, visible world. God has a plan not only for the resurrection of humankind but also for the redemption of creation. In truth, human beings know no other kind of life except bodily existence. Even if the most sophisticated dissecting tools imaginable could be fabricated, the soul could not be teased out of the body. The human creature is an indivisible unity of body, soul, mind, and spirit. Those of us struggling with issues of self-worth or self-image can recognize the value of their bodies and their lives because God values each human life. For all of us, how we live our lives, use our bodies, spend our time, and care for creation can be a testimony to our belief in the resurrection of the body.

Human destiny is bound to Christ's destiny. As he was born into a human body that would be raised, so are we.

Chapter 35

ALL SHALL BE MADE ALIVE
(1 Corinthians 15:21–22)

46. Chorus

Since by man came death,
by man came also
the resurrection of the dead.
For as in Adam all die,
even so in Christ
shall all be made alive.
> (1 Cor. 15:21–22)

1 Corinthians 15:21–23, 35–50

[21]For since death came through a human being, the resurrection of the dead has also come through a human being; [22]for as all die in Adam, so all will be made alive in Christ. [23]But each in his own order: Christ the first fruits, then at his coming those who belong to Christ. . . .

[35]But someone will ask, "How are the dead raised? With what kind of body do they come?" [36]Fool! What you sow does not come to life unless it dies. [37]And as for what you sow, you do not sow the body that is to be, but a bare seed, perhaps of wheat or of some other grain. [38]But God gives it a body

as he has chosen, and to each kind of seed its own body. [39]Not all flesh is alike, but there is one flesh for human beings, another for animals, another for birds, and another for fish. [40]There are both heavenly bodies and earthly bodies, but the glory of the heavenly is one thing, and that of the earthly is another. [41]There is one glory of the sun, and another glory of the moon, and another glory of the stars; indeed, star differs from star in glory.

[42]So it is with the resurrection of the dead. What is sown is perishable, what is raised is imperishable. [43]It is sown in dishonor, it is raised in glory. It is sown in weakness, it is raised in power. [44]It is sown a physical body, it is raised a spiritual body. If there is a physical body, there is also a spiritual body. [45]Thus it is written, "The first man, Adam, became a living being"; the last Adam became a life-giving spirit. [46]But it is not the spiritual that is first, but the physical, and then the spiritual. [47]The first man was from the earth, a man of dust; the second man is from heaven. [48]As was the man of dust, so are those who are of the dust; and as is the man of heaven, so are those who are of heaven. [49]Just as we have borne the image of the man of dust, we will also bear the image of the man of heaven.

[50]What I am saying, brothers and sisters, is this: flesh and blood cannot inherit the kingdom of God, nor does the perishable inherit the imperishable.

The relationship between the body and salvation was a source of tension in the Corinthian congregation. Those believers known as "enthusiasts" or "spiritualists" were abusing their bodies through debauchery (6:12), gluttony (6:13), and sexual immorality (6:15–20) under the cover of a misinterpretation of grace. They claimed that because they were already justified by grace (thus essentially already resurrected), what they did in their temporal bodily state did not matter.

This emphasis on body and soul was not likely Handel's concern when he devoted six-and-a-half movements to passages from Paul's extended discourse in 1 Corinthians 15. Overall, these texts paint a glorious picture of Judgment Day, when death will be defeated, Christ will reign eternal, and all humanity will be raised together to sing praise. Handel is not concerned with Paul's theological minutiae, but as believers seeking the way of salvation, we may benefit from exploring with Paul this complicated relationship between body and soul and in particular for this movement, the comparison of humanity to both Adam and to Christ, the "new Adam."

First, Paul rejects any simplistic materialism that would claim that the exact same earthly body that dies is resurrected. The rotting corpse in the grave is certainly not the resurrected body. But while Paul rejects the notion that the same physical body that believers possess on earth is raised, he is even more insistent that humans are raised with some type of body. Paul clearly does not see the body as inherently evil, as did Platonists and later Christian Manicheists. In 1 Thessalonians 5:23 Paul entreats believers, "May your spirit and soul and body be kept sound and blameless at the coming of our Lord Jesus Christ." And to the Corinthian "spiritualists" he said, "Glorify God in your body" (1 Cor. 6:20).

How then do we understand his claim that "flesh and blood cannot inherit the kingdom" (15:50)? It is too simplistic to say, as some commentators do, that "flesh" represents the physical, sensual part of humanity that does not enter the kingdom while "body" represents the wholeness of our being that does enter the kingdom. The better distinction is between life according to the flesh and life according to the spirit. "If you live according to the flesh [*kata sarka*], you will die; but if by the Spirit [*de pneumati*] you put to death the deeds of the body, you will live" (Rom. 8:13). Embodied life is not evil. What is evil is life according to the flesh/sinful nature (Gk.: *sarx*), a life in opposition to God's will, one that places confidence in earthly things and human achievements. So when Paul says that "flesh and blood cannot enter the kingdom," he is saying that an attitude *kata sarka* (according to the flesh) has no place in the presence of a holy and righteous God.

"Of the dust" and "of heaven" represent a similar distinction, not between the spiritual and the physical, since both Adam and Christ are embodied beings, but between Adam who follows the sinful nature (*sarx*) and Christ who follows the way of the Spirit. God, who created all things, from Adam to Jesus' infant body to you and me, can redeem the body "as he has chosen." Embodiment is a good thing. Christ, the logos, became embodied and walked among us, and contrary to the heretical line of preaching that endures in Christianity, salvation does not involve redemption *from* the body but redemption *of* the body.

Christ is the model for believers' resurrection. Christ's resurrected body is both like and unlike his earthly body, recognizable to believers but also transformed. Similarly, the resurrected bodies of believers will be identifiable but transformed, from the image of Adam to the image of Christ. Christ is "from heaven"; Adam is "from the dust." Again, this is not a contrast between embodiment and

disembodied spirituality but between ways of living. Just as
Adam represents a life lived according to the flesh, Christ
models the fruits of the Spirit. Believers simply partake of
Christ's resurrection. "Just as we have borne the image
of the man of dust, we will also bear the image of the man
of heaven" (v. 49). We "put on" Christ (Rom. 13:14) and
are "conformed to the body of his glory" (Phil. 3:21). Just
as we are the body of Christ on earth, at death we shall put
on the imperishable and immortal body of Christ.

Chapter 36

WE SHALL BE CHANGED
(1 Corinthians 15:51–53)

47. Accompanied Recitative

Bass
Behold, I tell you a mystery;
we shall not all sleep,
but we shall all be changed,
in a moment,
in the twinkling of an eye,
at the last trumpet.

　　　　　(1 Cor. 15:51–52)

48. Air

Bass
The trumpet shall sound,
and the dead shall be raised incorruptible,
and we shall be changed.
For this corruptible must put
on incorruption and this mortal
must put on immortality.

　　　　　(1 Cor. 15:52–53)

1 Corinthians 15:51–53

[51]Listen, I will tell you a mystery! We will not all die,
but we will all be changed, [52]in a moment, in the twin-

kling of an eye, at the last trumpet. For the trumpet will sound, and the dead will be raised imperishable, and we will be changed. [53]For this perishable body must put on imperishability, and this mortal body must put on immortality.

*E*veryone loves a good mystery, right? At the close of 1 Corinthians 15, Paul lets readers in on one. For us, "mystery" might suggest an enigma, puzzle, or intriguing problem, perhaps a crime, arousing suspense until a reasoned solution can be teased out. For Paul, *mysterion* refers, rather, to the hidden counsel or purposes of God, knowable not through reasoned problem solving but through revelation, proclamation, or fulfillment. Throughout chapter 15, Paul argues for the bodily resurrection of the dead, convinced that Christ's resurrection was not an exception but the crucial precedent for believers. At one point, his perspective is cosmic, surveying eschatological events leading to Christ's defeat of all powers hostile to God (vv. 24–28). At another, he underscores the personal consequences of there being no resurrection: "If for this life only we have hoped in Christ, we are of all people most to be pitied" (v. 19). "We" language returns in verses 51–58 as Paul proclaims the mystery of believers' ultimate release from mortality not in extinction but in transformation: "We will not all die, but we will all be changed."

This impending change is at the heart of his resurrection theology. In becoming one with creation in the incarnation, God is renewing or re-creating creation itself. More precisely, "resurrection" is synonymous with "re-creation" rather than with immortality. Paul wrote in 2 Corinthians 5:17, "If anyone is in Christ, there is a new creation: everything old has passed away; see, everything has become new!"

With verse 51, "We will not all die, but we will all be changed," many wonder whether Paul thought he or some of his hearers would be alive when Christ returned. Perhaps he did. Paul may also have used "we" more flexibly to include both present and future believers, holding that Christ's return would interrupt human history sooner or later. Clearly, however, transformation is promised equally to the living and the dead. Change will be sudden, happening in the smallest conceivable bit of time—as fast as the glance, sparkle, blink, or quiver of an eye. Yet a deliberate signal will announce it: a trumpet sound. In the Hebrew Bible, the sounding of a trumpet puts the listener on alert. It can signal the advent of war and violence (Jer. 4:19), the beginning of a time of communal prayer and fasting (Joel 2:15), and the coming of a king (1 Kgs. 1:34). Often, too, the sounding of a trumpet signals the presence or the advent of God (Exod. 19:16–20; Ps. 47:5; Joel 2:1); Paul is principally referring to this kind of sounding.

In referring to the "last" trumpet, he signals that such a sound will usher in the end of this age and the beginning of the age to come. This then is an eschatological mystery— a mystery about the end of our age and the beginning of the age of Christ. But in Paul's day, it must also have been understood in its military connotation, as the age of the coming of the one who would replace even the power of Rome itself, the coming of the one crucified by Rome, whom the Christians had the nerve to call Lord. Such a reversal is an important element of the mystery, for it underscores the commitment Paul had: not to the governing powers as they currently were, but to the ultimate governance of Jesus as Christ and thus as Lord.

It is more than a change in empire. It is a change of universal proportions—Christ takes his seat on the eternal throne, and the material world is transformed, from the waters of chaos down to our own flesh and blood. That which is perishable, subject to decay and destruction, and that which is mortal must put on, like clothing, imperishability and immortality. What one has previously been is not annihilated but subsumed into a state of being without previous vulnerabilities.

Our euphemism for death, "to pass away," is in fact dead on. "To pass away" suggests a change, a loss. According to Paul, what is lost will be our old existence, and all will lose that, whether they die before the Day of Judgment or not. "The dead [those who have passed away] will be raised imperishable, and we [who have not yet passed away] will be changed." The "old us" will pass away, as has already happened for those who have died, and all of us, who will all be "dead to sin" (Rom. 6:11), will put on immortality, a "new us," ready for the new age of Christ.

Chapter 37
DEATH, WHERE IS THY STING?
(1 Corinthians 15:54–58)

49. Recitative

Alto
Then shall be brought to pass
the saying that is written:
"Death is swallowed up in victory."
(1 Cor. 15:54)

50. Duet

Alto & Tenor
O death, where is thy sting?
O grave, where is thy victory?
The sting of death is sin,
and the strength of sin is the law.
(1 Cor. 15:55–56)

51. Chorus

But thanks be to God,
who giveth us the victory
through our Lord Jesus Christ.
(1 Cor. 15:57)

1 Corinthians 15:54-58

[54]When this perishable body puts on imperishability, and this mortal body puts on immortality, then the saying that is written will be fulfilled:
"Death has been swallowed up in victory."
[55]"Where, O death, is your victory?
    Where, O death, is your sting?"
[56]The sting of death is sin, and the power of sin is the law. [57]But thanks be to God, who gives us the victory through our Lord Jesus Christ.

[58]Therefore, my beloved, be steadfast, immovable, always excelling in the work of the Lord, because you know that in the Lord your labor is not in vain.

*P*aul's words spit in the face of death and also in the face of the grave. The King James Version, and thus *Messiah*, give these verses the earthiness they deserve: "Death is swallowed up in victory. O death, where *is* thy sting? O grave, where *is* thy victory?" (vv. 54–55). Or as a classic Easter hymn puts it, "Low in the grave he lay, Jesus my Savior . . . [but] Up from the grave he arose! With a mighty triumph o'er his foe; He arose a victor from the dark domain." He arose, and so shall we!*

When Christ returns and the physically dead and the spiritually dead put off perishability, decay, and sin and put on the imperishable body of Christ, then death will be totally "swallowed up in victory." This reference to the eschatological expectation of Isaiah 25 is the only time that

---

* Robert Lowry, "Low in the Grave He Lay," in *United Methodist Hymnal* (Nashville: The United Methodist Publishing House, 1989), 322.

Paul quotes an unfulfilled prophetic vision, but so sure is he
that in the new creation death has been decisively defeated
on the cross that he taunts the "final enemy" by asking,
"Where, O death, is your victory? Where, O death, is your
sting?" Often we read these as rhetorical questions, to the
point we don't even notice Paul's answer to his own taunt:
"The sting of death is sin."

The proper exegesis of this verse depends on one's
understanding of the nature of death. Some commentators claim that Paul is saying that physical death is the
result of sin; that humans were intended to live forever,
but sin introduces death to an otherwise immortal creation. But this is not the way in which Paul views death.
To understand what Paul means when he says that death
has "lost its sting" or that the "wages of sin is death"
(Rom. 4:23), we must first understand Paul's dialectical
view of death.

For Paul, two views of death stand in tension: death
as natural and death as final enemy. First, death represents
the natural end of human life. We are mortal beings, never
intended to live forever: "like grass that is renewed in the
morning; in the morning it flourishes . . . in the evening it
fades and withers" (Ps. 90:5–6). Death may be a cause of
regret for the dying and a source of mourning for the survivors, but it is not evil; it is simply the intended ending point
of our creaturely lives.

Paul claims, though, that "the last enemy to be
destroyed is death" (1 Cor. 15:26). How do we make
sense of this twofold vision, that death is both natural and
an enemy to be overcome? To do so, we must understand
what death means. Death entails alienation or separation on
three planes: from our bodies, from other human beings,
and from God. Life means unity with self, neighbor, and

God. Death threatens separation in all of its stark, horrific manifestations.

Thinking of death in terms of separation helps us understand how the two conceptions of death—as natural and as final enemy—are connected. In a world without sin, death is simply the natural end of human life, the closing of the first act of human existence. This should be followed by eternal life with God, because sin has not separated us from God. Because of sin, however, physical death threatens eternal separation from self, community, and, worst of all, God. Death is not something that happens only at the end of our physical existence. Because sin disrupts relationships, even though we are physically "alive," we are dying. The alienation of spiritual death is a potential precursor to the final separation following physical death. It is in this spiritual sense that Paul talks of being "dead through [our] trespasses and sins," separated from God and one another (Eph. 2:1).

The relationship between death as natural and death as the final enemy is now clearer. It is not that with sin previously immortal beings become mortal but, rather, that sin causes death to be a terror, threatening us with eternal separation. Without sin, death has no "sting"; it is simply a transition to eternal life with God.

Paul reminds us that we can be physically alive but spiritually dead. More important, we can attain eternal life not just when we physically die but also here and now. If spiritual death means separation, eternal life is the life of fellowship and love of God and neighbor. This is such good news that Paul breaks forth in doxology in verse 57: "Thanks be to God" that death, both the Redeemer's and the believers', has been defeated, "swallowed up" by Christ's victory on the cross.

Chapter 38

IF GOD BE FOR US
(Romans 8:31–39)

52. Air

Soprano or Alto
If God be for us,
who can be against us?
    (Rom. 8:31)

Who shall lay anything to the charge of God's elect?
It is God that justifieth,
who is he that condemneth?
It is Christ that died, yea rather,
that is risen again,
who is at the right hand of God,
who makes intercession for us.
                    (Rom. 8:33–34)

Romans 8:31–39

[31]What then are we to say about these things? If God is for us, who is against us? [32]He who did not withhold his own Son, but gave him up for all of us, will he not with him also give us everything else? [33]Who will bring any charge against God's elect? It is God who justifies. [34] Who is to condemn? It is Christ Jesus, who died, yes, who was raised, who is at the right hand of God, who indeed intercedes for us.

³⁵Who will separate us from the love of Christ? Will hardship, or distress, or persecution, or famine, or nakedness, or peril, or sword? ³⁶As it is written,
"For your sake we are being killed all day long;
we are accounted as sheep to be slaughtered."
³⁷No, in all these things we are more than conquerors through him who loved us. ³⁸For I am convinced that neither death, nor life, nor angels, nor rulers, nor things present, nor things to come, nor powers, ³⁹nor height, nor depth, nor anything else in all creation, will be able to separate us from the love of God in Christ Jesus our Lord.

*A*s the Christmas season draws to a close—our tree now brittle, our cookies a little stale, and our vacation days spent—we may feel a sense of malaise, articulated in the words "Back to the old grind." The final days of Christmas, bittersweet as they may be, are a good reminder of what it means for the Messiah to have come. We are invited to think about what difference Christ's advent here has made in the world and will make in our lives.

In the final section of Romans 8 Paul cheers on the Christians at Rome, reminding them that "if God is for us, who is against us?" (v. 31). The tone is emotional and celebratory. The marathon runners are at the halfway mark, and Paul reminds them and us that God has already made it to the end of the race, and God has won. With God's help, we too can make it to the finish line and participate in God's victory. Here Paul establishes the firm foundation that will empower and strengthen Jesus' followers during the hard work ahead of them, when the crowds are gone and the race-day decorations removed.

This is a helpful passage to read during periods of significant challenge and loss. It is often heard in the context of a Christian funeral. When Paul expresses his personal conviction—that he is convinced that nothing can separate us from the love of God in Christ Jesus—his statement is itself persuasive. Where the power of death is palpable, one can see how moved those gathered can be by Paul's words. Death is not the end but the beginning of a new phase of life in God. Funerals, however, are not the only places we mark grief and loss, as daily life has plenty of challenges and anxieties of its own.

Fortunately, this text speaks not solely of death but of many matters that threaten separation. Separation is a genuine issue in our lives. Every choice we make along the way necessarily separates us from some other option. One cannot become an adult without leaving childhood behind. One does not stay young forever, and so we leave behind our young adulthood with all its brimming potential. Nearly everyone understands that in the usual course of things, one's parents will die before he or she does. We raise our own children with a full expectation that they will go away from us, step out on their own. At the very heart of what it means to be human is separation from those things and those people we love. To be human is to have loss and grief. No one is able to escape loss and grief. Anyone who has remotely loved anyone or anything will suffer the grief of loss and will know the painful power of separation.

Portrayal of the powers that cause separation is part of the genius of the eighth chapter of Romans. Paul understands the conflict of cosmic forces that cause separation. He lists many of these forces. One of the first he mentions is hardship. Because it is included in a long list, it is easy enough to pass over lightly; but hardship should not be passed over lightly. Life is hard. The hardness of life, the struggles of work, health, and finances—for some more than others—are difficult to ignore.

Paul's list of those things that separate includes distress. Distress is a frequent force in our lives. When we cannot complete what we so want to finish, we are in distress. When we have done all that we can do, and it is still not enough, we are in distress. Like the waters flowing over a sinking ship, distress overwhelms us.

Paul goes on, naming "persecution, or famine, or nakedness, or peril, or sword." The forces that cause separation are many. The weight of all the forces that bring separation into our lives would appear to tip a scale completely over. But emboldened by Christ's justification and intercession, Paul proclaims to these powers loudly and firmly, "No." Shall these things prevail? Shall these things have the capacity to undo us, to undo the most central element of our lives—God's love? No, no, no! Paul makes a confession. He is convinced, he says, that nothing will prevail against God's love. The conflict of the powers is engaged head on, and the victor is God's love.

Chapter 39

WORTHY IS THE LAMB
(Revelation 5:11–13)

53. Chorus (Part 1)

Worthy is the Lamb that was slain,
and hath redeemed us to God by His blood,
to receive power, and riches, and wisdom,
and strength, and honour, and glory, and blessing.
Blessing and honour, glory and power,
be unto Him that sitteth upon the throne,
and unto the Lamb, for ever and ever.

(Rev. 5:12–13)

Revelation 5:11–13

[11]Then I looked, and I heard the voice of many angels surrounding the throne and the living creatures and the elders; they numbered myriads of myriads and thousands of thousands, [12]singing with full voice,
"Worthy is the Lamb that was slaughtered
to receive power and wealth and wisdom and might
and honor and glory and blessing!"
[13]Then I heard every creature in heaven and on earth and under the earth and in the sea, and all that is in them, singing,
"To the one seated on the throne and to the Lamb

be blessing and honor and glory and might
forever and ever!"

*A*t the culmination of *Messiah*, Handel takes us back to the
heavenly throne room where the angelic host sang, "Hallelujah!" This time, every creature in heaven and earth
and in all the seas sings together, worshiping God. This
crowd does not include just some creatures. It includes all
creatures, including those from under the earth, in Hades,
and in the sea that is known for its roiling chaos: "Then
I looked, and I heard the voice of many angels surrounding the throne and the living creatures and the elders; they
numbered myriads of myriads and thousands of thousands,
singing with full voice."

John's vision offers a comprehensive picture of inclu-
sivity—which may not be exactly what those who want to
separate the chaff from the wheat, the goats from the lambs,
and the good from the bad want to hear. There is no description of a bloody judgment day here. One of the challenges
of the text, then, is to read it in light of what has presumably
come before it. Many may prefer to focus on God's judgment and division. Yet these verses in Revelation describe
the culmination of the gospel story, begun so long before
with a baby in a manger and in promises spoken long before
that. In the scene before us we see what God's final word
will be—and it is not about division. Instead, it is about the
great myriads and myriads and thousands and thousands
surrounding the throne of God. Numbers like those do not
speak of separation and damnation. Instead, they describe
the gathering together of every creature in heaven and on
earth—and even under the earth, where some of the faithful might argue the most terrible of terrible creatures reside.

Yet even those who come from under the earth and from the great turmoil of the sea have voices with which to praise: "To the one seated on the throne and to the Lamb be blessing and honor and glory and might forever and ever!"

This passage carries a great message of comfort to the broken. God is able to work through suffering, for there is powerful consolation here for those who know brokenness. In Revelation 7:14, we learn that "'these are they who have come out of the great ordeal; they have washed their robes and made them white in the blood of the Lamb.'" This is why they are before the throne of God, rising to the promise that "'God will wipe away every tear from their eyes'" (7:17).

In all of our brokenness, we are never too damaged for God to use us. The gospel, the entire story of a king being born in a lowly stable, rejected and crowned with thorns, redefines what it means to "win," and here in the throne room we are reminded again how the cross has changed our understanding of victory. Victory is not reserved for those who do the wounding (or who manage to escape being wounded). Victory is given to the wounded, leading us to learn that it is not through our own physical power or our triumph over others that we win anything. Only in God are we made worthy. Recognizing the worthiness of the Lamb that was slaughtered, we find our own path to worthiness. Insecure, self-doubting human beings cannot hear that message too many times.

Christ's advent among us demonstrates that ultimate power does not belong to those who appear most powerful but instead to those who appear wounded and broken like the Lamb. Despite all of our inclinations to think otherwise, that means every one of us. Like it or not, we are all invited to be part of the glorious choir of those singing praise and honor to God both now and in the moment of final victory.

Chapter 40
AMEN
(Revelation 5:14)

53. Chorus (Part 2)

Amen.
(Rev. 5:14)

Revelation 5:14

[14]And the four living creatures said, "Amen!" And the elders fell down and worshiped.

*W*hen he decided to propose to his girlfriend, Isaac Lamb went all out, organizing his friends and family (and maybe even some professionals) to help him pull off a choreographed flash-mob proposal. The video went viral on YouTube as millions of strangers were amazed and inspired by Isaac's over-the-top way of popping the question. A few months after the wedding, Isaac called his loved ones together again to create another choreographed ode to love, marriage, and family.

To a soundtrack of Stefano's song "Yes to Love," the video tells the story of how each set of Isaac's grandparents met, wed, and raised large families. Family members held enlarged photos of the matriarchs and patriarchs, kissed, and danced around, celebrating the two couples' combined fourteen children, forty grandchildren, and thirty-five great-grandchildren. The message is clear: all these people, all these relationships, and all this joy are the result of those two couples saying yes to love.

Anyone who has been married knows that such a commitment is no simple yes, like someone would reply to a question like "Would you like fries with that?" Rather, it is an affirmation of hope, an earnest agreement to a proposed plan—in effect, it is an amen.

Amen is a Hebrew word meaning "So be it." *The New Interpreter's Dictionary of the Bible* defines it as "a term of ratification," like a stamp of approval on what has been spoken. In the case of Revelation 5, it is the four creatures (first described in Rev. 4:6–8) affirming the words of honor and praise that the whole world has spoken: "So be it. Yes. Let there indeed be blessing and honor and glory and power to the Lamb forever and ever." In worship or prayer, we close with "Amen" to affirm our commitment to and trustworthiness in what has been sung or said. The writer of Revelation ends his letter with "Amen," affirming the visions he has shared and his expression of grace to those who receive his letter. Handel closes *Messiah* with "Amen," affirming both the song of praise just quoted from Revelation 5 and the entire oratorio, Handel's song of praise to a mighty and glorious God.

With conclusions like these, we might be tempted to consider "Amen" an end when really it is a beginning. Our "So be it" should not be a passive wish that what has been spoken will be fulfilled but a giant yes to participating in the work of God. Such a commitment is lived out in the little things of a faithful life—showing compassion, acting with integrity—and in the more life-altering leaps of faith to which God might call you. The costs of saying yes to God may be unknown, but the rewards are as well.

When Isaac Lamb's grandparents met, fell in love, and said yes to a lifetime partnership, they could not have known how many progeny would result or what kinds of trials and joys they would experience, but they said yes based on confidence in the one to whom they were making such a commitment. When Mary told the angel Gabriel, "Yes. Let it be with me as you have said," she could not have known all that would lie in store for her and her child. When Joseph said yes to marrying a woman others deemed unfaithful, and yes to fathering a child that was not biologically his own, he could not have known what a frightful and thrilling journey lay in their future.

But in faith, Mary said yes. Joseph said yes. John said yes to a supporting role, preparing the way for his Savior. Jesus said yes to sorrow and suffering on behalf of a sinful world. And as disciples, we say yes to following Christ, giving honor to God, accepting the callings God speaks into our lives.

Our celebration of the Messiah's coming does not end with a date on the calendar. We celebrate Christ's birth, teaching, triumph over death, and eternal reign every day, affirming his worthiness with our lives. As disciples, we live a life of saying yes to God. A life of amen.

LIST OF CONTRIBUTORS

The majority of the reflections in this volume are excerpted and adapted from essays in the *Feasting on the Word* commentary series. Those essays were written by the following scholars and pastors, to whom we give our thanks.

Thomas L. Are Jr.
Deborah A. Block
Kathleen Long Bostrom
James T. Butler
Katherine C. Calore
Charles Campbell
Gary W. Charles
Kate Colussy-Estes
Noel Leo Erskine
Kyle D. Fedler
Dana Ferguson
Roger A. Ferlo
Terence E. Fretheim
Lewis F. Galloway
Daniel Harris
Martha C. Highsmith
Aaron Klink
Gregory H. Ledbetter
B. Diane Lipsett

Kimberly Bracken Long
Ellen Ott Marshall
Donald K. McKim
Seth Moland-Kovash
Rodger Y. Nishioka
Kathleen M. O'Connor
Lance Pape
Stephanie A. Paulsell
Blair Alison Pogue
Stephen G. Ray Jr.
Nelson Rivera
John D. Rohrs
Don E. Saliers
David J. Schlafer
Richard L. Sheffield
Richard F. Ward
Andrea Wigodsky
Patrick J. Wilson